HAPPIER THAN THIS DAY AND TIME

An Oral History of the Outer Banks of North Carolina

Collected and with an Introduction by David Poyer

Northampton House Press

HAPPIER THAN THIS DAY AND TIME: An Oral History of the Outer Banks of North Carolina. © 2012 by David Poyer. All rights reserved. Brief excerpts may be quoted for use in reviews or for purposes of scholarship, if attributed.

    Cover credits: Upper left photograph, lifesaving operations, circa 1907; public domain. Upper right, Wright Brothers Flight No. 46, public domain. Lower, A. H. Gray store at Waves, D. Victor Meekins Collection, Outer Banks History Center, Manteo NC; by permission. Cover design by Naia Poyer.

    Published by Northampton House LLC. ISBN 978-1481089-43-2.

    First edition, second printing.

Acknowledgments

Ex nihilo nihil fit. This project required the willing help of dozens of people on and off the Banks. Deserving of special mention and thanks are Natalie Case-Austin, Allen Graham, Naomi Hester, Michael McOwen, Gee Gee Rosell, Beth Storie, Levin Stowe, Mrs. L.J. Shannon, Reverend Spotswood Graves, Manson Meekins, Charles Gray, Lin Poyer, Mae Fulcher, and Palmyra Midgett. Additional thanks more recently to Sarah Downing and KaeLi Schurr of the Outer Banks History Center, and to my daughter, Naia Poyer.

And of course, above all, to our oral sources. All errors and omissions are my own.

HAPPIER THAN THIS DAY AND TIME

Is there any thing whereof it may be said, See, this is new? It hath been already of old time, which was before us.

–Ecclesiastes 1:10

CONTENTS

Introduction:
A Dike against Oblivion   1

Little Barefoot Girl:
Maggie Mae Twiford   12

I Done What I Set Out to Do:
Captain Ernal Foster   22

A Life In Manteo:
Benjamin Allen Creef   35

Curiosity Lane:
Elizabeth Ann O'Neal Howard   51

I May Become an Educated Man:
Nicholas Longworth Meekins   62

Remember, We Don't Give Up:
Marilyn Daniels Midgett   83

I'll Do What I Can:
Roland Francis Stowe   98

Looking Out For M'self:
Inez Gaimel Beacham   117

Afterword   135

INTRODUCTION:
A Dike against Oblivion

How much would you give to talk quietly for just one hour with your great-grandmother?

Most likely, almost anything. But probably you can't buy it at any price. Time's torrent rushes by, isolating us like a hurricane-driven tide, the rising sea cutting us off from those who went before. It bears away before we know it the old voices and the old ways. Bears away too much of what we loved, and what we realize, too late, we still desperately need.

This book's a bridge back to that past. In these few pages eight men and women recount their lives on the isolated barrier islands of the North Carolina coast. They tell of childhood, courting, marriage, and children; of hurricanes, depressions, wars, and death; of faith, doubt, love, and fear.

Most of those whose voices you'll hear are poor or obscure. Yet they are all extraordinary. Now, near the end of their voyages, they linger yet for a little while to tell us of The Way Things Were.

And they will tell us more – if we'll listen. With a little urging, they'll tell us their thoughts on the ultimate questions; good and evil, youth and age, triumph and suffering. From their first word, they cast a spell.

Welcome to the past.

The Outer Banks

This book is about eight very special individuals, more than it's about a single time or place. But it's also important to understand where they came from. Because it is a place apart, separated in space and time from today's America, and even from today's South.

The Outer Banks of North Carolina are a rampart the land has thrown up against the sea. They are a hundred-mile arch of barrier islands, about twelve feet above sea level, from a few thousand feet to three miles across and punctuated by narrow inlets to the Atlantic. Low, backed by wide brackish sounds, they are lands of the margin; half-land, half-sea; open through their history to the systole and diastole of the tide, shaped by the eternal struggle of sea-currents, vulnerable to hurricane and war.

In the 1580's these islands' Native American inhabitants defeated the first English attempt to colonize the New World at Roanoke Island. But later they retreated, decimated by new diseases, new weapons, and new ways of life. The Banks were permanently settled by second-generation colonists trickling down from Jamestown, Williamsburg, and Norfolk, leavened with fugitives from the King's justice, retired pirates, and shipwrecked mariners. These were the direct ancestors of today's numerous Baums, Burrises, Etheridges, Grays, Howards, Manns, Midgetts, O'Neals, Perrys, Stowes, Tillets, Twifords, and other old and famous families.

These early settlers located at the islands' widest points, where shelter from salt-carrying wind and storm-driven surge is best. Even there, however, the Banks are mostly sand (except for Roanoke Island), which means that crop size and type are limited. So they looked to the sea for their livelihood, and carried on coastal trade for their staples, tools, and their few luxuries.

The Banks were on the front lines in the Revolution and the War of 1812. But soon after that the transition to steamboat and rail relegated them to the backwaters of commerce. From trade, piloting, shipbuilding, and occasional piracy and wrecking, the Bankers turned to fishing, waterfowl hunting, and subsistence farming. The Civil War interrupted their isolation for a time. Several of the early battles were fought here, and Roanoke Island was a Federal garrison and a haven for liberated slaves. But once again history moved on, and their way of life was unaltered.

The immigration that changed American demography in the latter half of the nineteenth century had less effect in the South than in the North, and practically none on the Banks. Like certain areas of the Ozarks, these islands remained ethnically English and Welsh. Their spoken language still reflects this, though it's being attenuated now under the twin onslaughts of resortization and electronic entertainment.

But the people you'll meet in a moment lived most of their lives before these onslaughts came. They grew to adulthood in an isolated, relatively simple rural society. There were no paved roads; no railroads; no cars; no airplanes; no telephones; no electricity.

More than technology has changed since then. The very structure of social intercourse was different. Law was less intrusive, and the restraints of family and religion more universally accepted and effective than today. There was little assistance available from government, but neighbors helped one another in time of need. Black and white lived apart, but segregation was tempered to some degree by traditional forms of interaction: common employments, a certain courtesy, and not least the mutual dependence hard to avoid on isolated islands.

Then, of course, came the automobile, the watershed between the nineteenth and twentieth-century worlds. Yet they too came late here; there wasn't a complete road though the Banks till the early nineteen-fifties, and free access to the outer world didn't come till 1964 with the building of a bridge over Oregon Inlet. (Reaching Ocracoke Island still requires nearly an hour on a ferry.) Electricity too was a latecomer. Kerosene lamps were common on the Banks till the nineteen-thirties, and families still fill them when a hurricane builds to southward. Television arrived on southern Hatteras only in the nineteen-eighties.

These older people of the Banks, then, are in a sense the last survivors of nineteenth-century America. They were born into a world of large families and early deaths; into an economy dependent on natural resources exploitable with simple technology but great skill. Most of them have worked hard all their lives. This shows in their hands, in their faces, and in their attitudes toward life.

As it happens, they also have a strong sense of history. All of them were raised in an oral tradition, usually of the Bible, but all of spoken story.

What this means, ethnic and geographic stasis combined with an oral tradition, is that the Outer Banks hold one of the richest lodes of oral tradition left in the United States.

It's sad that no one has, until very recently, bothered to collect and publish it. (But probably we could say this at any given time; the dikes against oblivion require constant repair.) Noteworthy previous efforts were the work of the Currituck Historical Society, the definitive books of David Stick, and the Sea Chest magazine published by Hatteras High School at Buxton. But what you hold in your hands now is the first book-length collection of oral reminiscences from the Outer Banks.

We're glad we did it. We've been richly rewarded. We've met the most fascinating people of our lives.

The Utility of Reminiscence

Why did we undertake a project like this? Does the world really need another book?

We think so. Because we think autobiography is important. And reminiscence is the autobiography of the common man.

The passing down of story from generation to generation takes place in all cultures we know of. Aside from being entertaining, it is an essential element in the socialization of the young. In our age it's fallen on hard times, another victim of mass entertainment. But we think it's even more valuable today. Along with fiction, a closely related realm of writing, it accomplishes something that nothing else can. It is the only medium or device capable, at its best, of permitting us to step outside our individual selves and into those of others.

This has two effects. First, it teaches us that other people, no matter what they look or sound like, are as valuable and as deserving of respect, love, and mercy as ourselves. Every religion and philosophy recognizes this. Yet we need only look around us to see that the message bears repeating.

Second, through this identification with others, it can help a thoughtful reader to evolve a mature morality–that is, to become wise–more rapidly than through pure personal experience.

The people whose stories we are about to read have gone through this process. They've arrived at their own conclusions. They express them differently, some in terms of their religious creed, others in homespun homilies. But gradually we became aware that they were at least roughly congruent. This should surprise no one. As Flannery O'Connor, the Southern Catholic short-story writer, put it, "Everything that rises must converge." They reached them; but many admitted ruefully that they had gotten there the hard way.

We began collecting these interviews in the late nineteen-seventies, out of a vague sense that they were interesting, that they'd be fun to read. By 1982 the interview process was basically complete. Some of these texts appeared, in abbreviated versions, in a guidebook we were publishing on the Banks. But gradually we became convinced that these stories of hard and simple lives ought to reach a larger audience; and this is their first publication in whole, and all together.

We suspect that biography and the simple, homely wisdom of reminiscences – can speed us toward the same conclusions that we would reach much later on our own. Studying life through the lenses of older and wiser minds can spare us years of unhappiness and struggle. And since each of our evil acts leads to misery for others, like a chain letter with sorrow for the prize, it thus lessens the sum of suffering in the world.

On Method

A few words about how we gathered and edited these reminiscences may be in order. (For those who are interested, we'll discuss it in more depth in the Afterword.) Our usual work is novels, and we found both similarities and differences to the craft of fiction in doing this book.

The first challenge was locating sources. In many years of working and writing on the Banks, we'd noticed that it seemed everyone knew somebody who was eighty-five or ninety and still hale and active, still a great storyteller. Thus, we started with a good reserve of possible leads. However, when we tried to interview them we often found that, sadly, things had changed. Those were painful meetings. All we could do was sit with them for a while, hold their hands in sympathy, and then bid them farewell.

Once we identified sources, we had to gain their confidence. We therefore sincerely thank those residents we name in the Acknowledgements. They were willing to act as go-betweens, often on slight acquaintance, and a familiar name made our sources much more comfortable.

During the actual interviews, a primary rule was respect for the dignity of our older friends. Thus, we never pressed any issue. There were those, for example, who didn't want to discuss how black folk were treated early in the century. We had to balance their right to privacy against the interest readers would naturally have in certain material. Our approach, after much reflection, was to ask such questions again at the re-interview. Met with two silences or evasions we dropped the topic. Professional historians might not be satisfied with this approach, but we wanted to respect privacy above all.

We did many interviews that didn't pan out for various reasons. Those you'll read here were the best.

Once things were rolling, we partially guided the conversation, when it needed it, with brief and general leading questions. Though they often went in circles for hours, each conversation eventually progressed through three stages. The first recounted the source's family history and ended with birth or coming to consciousness. The second recounted their lives. And the third was a summing-up or statement of their philosophical, ethical, or religious conclusions.

Leading questions for the first stage were of this sort: How long has your family been here? Who were your mother's people? What is the first thing you remember?

For the second, the life-recounting: What games did you play growing up? When did you go to work? How did you meet your spouse? How did you feel when you lost your sight? How did you live during the Depression? Did you see ships sinking in the war? How did you raise your children?

The most difficult were those eliciting the summing-up portion of the interview. What was the happiest part of your life? The saddest? Is there anything you wish you had done? Is there anything you wish you hadn't done? What are your plans for the future? Do you think life has a purpose? Do you believe in an afterlife? Are you afraid to die?

For obvious reasons, these last were hard to ask sometimes. But they addressed one of our prime reasons for undertaking this book. More about this in a moment!

Finally, few of us can speak for publication without some editing. Our sources would, we felt, be ill-served by a completely unedited transcription. This called at last the novelist's ear into action, to condense without losing flavor or meaning, leaving intact the flow and feel of a distinctive and graceful speech. It's a demanding, time-consuming, but utterly absorbing process.

Some Tentative Conclusions

This book is not history in the academic sense. For that, no one will likely ever surpass David Stick's definitive histories of the Banks, especially *The Outer Banks of North Carolina* and *Graveyard of the Atlantic*, published by the University of North Carolina Press.

We call it, rather, "oral" history. This is not to impugn anyone's veracity. But this may be truth of a different kind; history as Homer practiced it, a compound of fact, art, myth, and most of all, wisdom from a lifetime of living.

Believing this, we did not check or "correct" our sources' testimony against published accounts or other records. We accepted that what they say is true in some sense; perhaps not always factually verifiable, but at the very least, true as a good story or poem is true.

As we said above, there was an ulterior motive in doing these interviews.

We began this project with a larger ambition than "simply" recording stories. St. Thomas Aquinas said, "Only the wise man is truly free;" Sophocles, "There is no happiness where there is no wisdom." All thinking beings struggle to answer certain questions. How can we be happy? How can we live full lives? What is our purpose here? Is there life after death?

Here we have eight people who've had a lifetime to ponder these questions. That's over five hundred years of life experience. Perhaps, we dared to think, they might have reached some useful conclusions.

So do they have answers, these old people? I suspect they do. They may not all explain them well. But philosophers and prophets have agreed down the ages that truth is possible to grasp, but hard to communicate. You must judge for yourself.

The Return

You're sitting out on the screened porch, in a rocking chair, looking out over the moonlit Pamlico. Or maybe you're not old enough for a chair, you're just sitting on the steps, listening to your great-grandparents chatting. You're looking up at the Dipper, listening to the wind sandpapering the shingles; the cicadas are fiddling hard out under the live oaks; from far off comes from time to time the lonely double bell of an anchored schooner, or maybe the sad distant drone of the old *Hattie Creef,* feeling her way through the channel home.

Let's go back....

LITTLE BAREFOOT GIRL:
Maggie Mae Twiford

The late November sunlight glints off the Nags Head dunes outside the window, and glints again off Maggie Twiford's snow-white hair. It is cut short and pinned up with a brown barrette. Her tiny hands lie softly together in the colorful afghan that covers her lap, except when they twist at the plastic band at her wrist. Outside in the corridor there is the hiss of wheelchairs on tile, the chatter of nurses.

"It was all dirt roads in them days. All such as that. And I remember a lot about it. My mother and my father have been dead for years, and my sisters and my brothers too. And I've got three relatives here, and all my other kinfolks are dead. I've got children – three, two boys and a girl. And today's my youngest son's birthday, he's 62 years old today.

"I was born in 1900. Our closest doctor was at Poplar Branch, Doctor Griggs. Had to go by water to get him, wa'n't no bridges, you see. Sometimes you died fore the doctor got there. My mother had a doctor, Doctor Newburn. He lived at Jarvisburg. And both of them was with my mother when I was born.

"Most all my people were Service people. My father was in the Coast Guard – it was the Lifesaving Service, years ago.

He was a surfman. I heard him say that his mother died when he was thirteen years old, and he couldn't go to school. He had to go out and work to take care of his mother; his daddy was dead. He had it pretty hard. I never heard him say what he did when he was a boy. I imagine he fished. T'weren't nothing else much to do here. He didn't have no education, that was the reason he couldn't get rated, couldn't get up. Well, he was a big stout man, and he had a red complexion. Oh, he was a wonderful father. And he didn't live too long after he was retired. But he was in the Service 37 years. I heard him say that when he went in the service it was at Number Nine station. That was Poyner's Hill. Then he was transferred to Paul Gamiels. Don't imagine there's anything left there now, they've had so many storms.

"My people come from Kitty Hawk. My people were Beals. B-E-A-L. Some B-E-A-L-E. We call ours B-E-A-L-S. Now my father I don't know where really he come from. Up in the hills...seems to me I've heard him say that his mother was from Columbia or somewhere over that way. Uh huh. My mother's family name is Perry. She was a Kitty Hawk Perry. They have a lot of Perrys in Kitty Hawk. Used to. There's a few still living but not as many as there was years ago. And my mother's mother, she was a Fisher. I think there were four of them, Fisher girls. My grandmother Betty, and Thanny, Amy, and Lebarcia. I didn't know them, that was before I was born. I didn't have no grandparents when I was small.

"My mother died having my sister, when I wasn't quite three years old. I don't remember what she looked like. I wish I had some faint remembrance of her but I don't. She's buried in Kitty Hawk. All my people are buried in Austin's Cemetery there.

"But my little sister lived to be grown and married. And she died the same way my mother died. And she had typhoid fever along with it, and of course the baby didn't live. There wasn't time for it to be borned. And my sister Martha, she died about the same way my mother died. In childbirth. And then my oldest sister died in 1919 of the flu, when it was raging, you know, so bad? She didn't live but one week from the time she was taken, went into pneumonia and died.

"My daddy was a hard workin' man. And he raised a big family. I had three sisters, and I had one, two, three – four brothers. There was eight of we children to raise up, and he in the service. He had to have a housekeeper to take care of us. No, not colored, elderly white women mostly. And I'm telling you he had a hard time of it.

"But he was a good father. Didn't make much money, but there was a lot of people didn't make as much as he did. We had something to eat and a place to stay in. He always worshipped we four girls.

"I was a little barefooted girl. In the summer I went barefoot. We had a little one-room schoolhouse in Duck. You wouldn't believe it to go up there now. There's a art gallery there now. And it was history, geography, arithmetic, things like that.

"We had ball games. We had a game we called fifty-oh. And ring around the roses. And a game we called sheepie. You'd be surprised at the silly things we had them days. How do you play fifty-oh? Some would go off and hide, and we'd try to find them. And if you found them and could make the home run before they did we'd win the game. Yes, hide and seek was what it was, and they called it fifty-oh then. We played cat, sure did. It's been so long ago I nearly forgot. And we had a croquet set, young people used to come to our lawn and play.

"And on Sunday afternoon we'd go to this big hill north of Duck. It wasn't as big as Jockey's Ridge, but it didn't lack much. And we'd run up and down it and play until we were so tired we couldn't hardly get back.

"We had one teacher that rang a bell – it was a hand bell. The teacher would stand in the door and ring, ring, when we children would be playing, for us to come in. And we had to stay in at recess a lot, we'd misbehave and done something we shouldn't. Whisperin' in school, or laughing. There was a lot of laughing. And certain ones had to stay and sweep the schoolroom and put things in order for next day. Went to school in the summertime, hot weather, barefoot – we didn't have to wear shoes, no.

"The Wright brothers? They flew in 1903. I was born in 1900. Oh, yes, they came back in 1908. I remember that. But there was always something going on that I didn't know about. I didn't really live that close to Kill Devil. I saw them flying around. It looked different from planes they have now. We thought it was something scary, flying around up there.

"My daddy had a horse that he used at the station, and then on his liberty at home. He'd bring the horse home. He didn't have but one day liberty a week, one day and one night. He come home at twelve and left next day at eleven to get back to the station. It was about a hour's ride on the horse because it was sand, it took longer to go. He had to be on time, they were strict them days. The horse was named Fanny. That horse ran away with him. I think he was on patrol and the horse got frightened, something happened that he just ran. And threw him out of the cart and hurt him pretty bad. Throwed him out on his head. Doctor had to tend him.

"Sometimes he patrolled with the horse, but most times he walked. He had what they call a lay-house on each end. Between the two stations, you know. And most times he had to walk the night. He had a north patrol, sometimes he had a south patrol. If it was a stormy night he'd patrol twice a night. And again he'd just have one patrol a night. He'd walk up and down the beach – that ocean had to be watched for ships, y'know. And I can remember all the ships come ashore when he was in there and I used to worry when I was a kid when I'd hear talk – we'd get word from the station there was a shipwreck on the beach, and I knew my daddy had to go. I remember how I used to worry about it, thought maybe he wouldn't make it back. Because then they said go, you didn't have to come back. It was the rule. If it was possible to get to the ship, to get the men off, they had to go. And sometimes you didn't come back. You got drowned. I remember seein' em come ashore. Ships from different countries. Some men got lost, some got saved. Some ships was torn to pieces. I've seen men washed ashore on the beach drowned. That's when I was a little girl.

"There wasn't very much. The houses weren't very well kept up. There weren't very many big homes. There were some hunting lodges, one or two. The people who weren't in the service depended on fishing.

"I'm telling you we had a rough time of it, but them were the happy days. Happier than they are in this day and time. We didn't have a lot, but what we had we enjoyed. And we didn't look for a whole lot. If I got a rag doll at Christmas, and a stocking full of nuts and candy and all that, I was happy with it. Now little children gets everything and in no time it's tore up and gone. We took care of our little things that we got.

"But we were happy people them days. It was almost like one big family. Some of them was poorer than others. And them that had a little bit more they'd always divide. I know my daddy did.

"My daddy never had much money but he always raised a lot of stuff to eat around him. Even guineas. And hogs. He had a lot of hogs. We didn't have to buy no meat, no lard. The hogs went free till the new law, the fence law come in, and he had to get rid of them. The woods used to be full of hogs and cattle. Always had a plenty to eat on Christmas. Wasn't like it is now – all beefsteak. We raised chickens and raised geese and ducks, we had fowls of all kinds. And then gunnin', you know, you killed wild ducks and geese. No problem 'bout eating. We had a garden and grew beans, and collards, and cabbage, sweet potatoes and horse potatoes, cucumbers, tomatoes, most every kind of vegetable you could raise around here. It wasn't the kind of food people eats this day and time. It was good food, it sure was.

"No, you wouldn't hardly believe how people lived them days. We only went to the city once a year. Elizabeth City, that was the closest city. That wasn't very big but to us it was a big one. It was like goin' to New York. Nobody got nowhere much – I think I did go to Norfolk once or twice when I was growin' up. Went on a steamboat. The Currituck, I think."I moved to Chesapeake in 1918. We didn't have no high school. I went there to take a business course. It was in Norfolk, on Main Street. Mr. Wresler's college. He died, and Mr. Keyes took it over.

"No, I didn't get a job then. I married William Twiford, in 1918, and he wouldn't let me go to work. He was from Princess Anne, there's where his people was from. He lived down Corolla. But we lived in Norfolk for right many years. My oldest son was born in South Norfolk, and my daughter was born in South Norfolk.

"Then we moved from Norfolk to Church's Island. He was a guide, for two lodges. White's, and for Hampton. Duck hunting lodges. Oh, yes, I know that's a unpleasant job – he complained about it. I think we were there a couple, three year he worked for the lodge. From there he put in for the Coast Guard. He decided he'd better when he was younger go in the service.

"And we were stationed in Dam Neck. And we lived there I think two year. From there we moved from one station to the other. And finally settled down in Duck, where I was born. And he was in Caffey's Inlet, and then in Kitty Hawk. And I think in Nags Head too. He was all over. And he went to Florida too, was there a whole winter. But I didn't go, the children was small. And he got transferred back. We were in Wash Woods I think six years. That's up above Corolla. And

Caffeys Inlet. I think he retired out of Kitty Hawk. He's been dead – buried him close to twenty year.

"I remember the worst hurricane up there was in 1933. You can't imagine what a hurricane sounds like. It's terrible – Whoooo. The water came up and flooded us out of our house. Everybody had to leave their home. First we went to the garage, on a hill, and there was lots of women and children in there. The ocean was between us and the station, and the surf had bursted their lifeboat all to pieces. So the men couldn't come and help us. We were helpless. And the water was rising. There was this old lady who had a big house, and she would take people in. The children wanted to go there. So to please the children I left the garage and was trying to get to it. Wading. But the water was too deep, and it was coming in, and I had to try to get up to the top of a hill. And it was sand, and I had the children by both my hands, trying to get up to the top of that sand hill. And I couldn't do it, and the water was rising. But just then the eye of the storm came and we was able to get to safety at the house.

"Some of the houses was took away – the ocean just took them away. I was lucky. The sand was hilled up as high as the eaves of my house. The wind was so strong it blew the winter lights and the curtains and the shades and the glass out, and blew some of the roof off. And the sea had eat under my kitchen. But I had my house. That's the reason I don't think much of the beach. I just look on that water and walk away. And I think that was why when I was growing up, my father kept us so far from the shore.

"Oh, yes, I really feel lucky to have my children. I got

five or six grandchildren. There's more than grandchildren, of great ones. I don't know how many I got, haven't counted them up lately. And I love the great ones just as good as I do the grandchildren.

"I've been in here for two years now. I'm not getting much better, but my mind seems to be clearer. But I'm a lot better than some of them in here. I'll tell you, this is a pitiful place. You go around and see the sufferin' and the sick people. I'm not bodily sick, but I broke my hip a couple of year ago and something happened that the leg got twisted. They did try to straighten it out, but I think they waited too long. It can't never be back right. And this wheelchair...I'm still not well. And I don't think I've got enough time for this hip to ever heal.

"This is a wonderful place to be. They have helicopters here, they take you to hospitals, to the doctors. I haven't been on them. We have everything here that's needed for this kind of home. And my children take care of me pretty good, they do all they can for me. But I'll be glad if I can get out.

"I've had a lot of trouble in my life, yes I have. I think the unhappiest time was when the children left home. I had two in the war. Clyde was in Germany, right in the midst of the battle there. He got his feet froze there. He still has trouble with his legs. And Tom was in the Navy, on the high seas the times when ships were getting sunk down here. You never knew when word was coming that he was drowned. I had a lot of worry on to me. You're bound to worry about them when they're facing danger every minute of their life. And Tom got rheumatic fever in England, and it still bothers him.

"The happiest time was when I was young – getting married, I reckon.

"The best way I'm happiest is when I know the Lord's going to take care of me. I know I've got to die. But while I'm living I feel like if I live the right life, which I try my best, then he'll take care of me. Although I'm suffering, that'll be over after a while. I want to be prepared to not have none of these aches and things. No, I'm not afraid, not a bit. I want to live as long as the Lord sees fit for me to live, then when it's time I got no dread. No worry about my soul. I know the Bible tells us a lot, but I still think we got to die and go on to find out really what it's all about. Maybe I'm wrong, but if I am it's ignorance, the Lord will forgive me."

Maggie Twiford sits facing the window, immobile in the waning sunlight, watching as the wind ruffles the beach grass at the top of a dune. If you were eight years old, barefoot, you could scramble to the top in a minute. And see for a long, long way.

I DONE WHAT I SET OUT TO DO:
Captain Ernal Foster

"Yep, I got to get cleaned up some in here one of these days."

Captain Ernal Foster looks slowly around the interior of what he calls his "equipment building." Against the walls are stacked bundles of hand-tied nets. In the roof beams are bamboo poles, rods, old outriggers striped red and white. Covering the plank floor are heaps of bronze propellers, fighting chairs, Pflueger Altapac reels, old cans of Athey and Pettit paint and varnish. "That's my father's sail bag over there, with his needles and palms. And his sea chest, there in the corner. One of these days. . . Come on, let's talk in the house."

The gray house on the sea side of Hatteras Village looks small and commonplace from Highway 12. But inside, its pine-paneled walls are covered with mounted marlin, sailfish, swordfish. The furniture is oak, from old ships; Hazel shows you a Singer that washed ashore in the 1890's. Even the bathroom doors came from a vanished schooner.

Foster is not a large man, but at 76 his shoulders still bulge under his loose shirt as he lowers himself into his armchair. The steady eyes are the color of a blue marlin's back. And then the only sound is the soft voice, and faintly from outside the endless crash of the surf.

"I was born and raised on this spot, spent most of my life here. My father, he was raised down here on this hill, but they claim his father was a Yankee. My mother was born and raised here. I grew up one of seven children. Three girls, four boys. I happened to be the oldest boy.

"When I grew up there wasn't much to do round here. We boys entertained ourselves. We had shove-skiffs we made – wasn't no harbor here then, we kept the boats out in the sound, on stakes, and you went back and forth with a shove-skiff. You didn't row, you had oars and you shoved back and forth. We boys, we sewed some sails out of these burlap bags. Them skiffs didn't have centerboards on them, they was flat-bottom – and on a northeast wind, we'd race down to the point beach, three or four miles, four or five of us. And then we'd shove back. If it was southwesterly we'd shove down there and race back home. And we had horses to chase and catch, and ride on the beach. And we played cat. How do you play cat? Take socks, and unravel the yarn and make a ball out of it. You throw the ball at the man, and if you hit him he'd be out. Didn't have no money for baseballs. We boys had teams. When anybody lost there'd be a fight. But we had games like that. I don't know how we could have had a better time.

"Then when we got to our teens boys and girls would get together at their homes, and get some cocoa, try and get some sugar, and we'd have a cook-candy. And some of the boys didn't get invited, when you'd set the candy out to cool they'd come around and steal it. When we did taffy you'd pull it out, a boy and a girl. If it didn't break she'd have candy in both hands and you could kiss her. Then on Fourth of July we'd take our boat and go to Ocracoke, to the dances. I had me a Ocracoke girl. Ever heard of Aycock Brown? He married my girl friend.

"My father started working me when I was a boy. He didn't let me lay around. When I was small, on Saturdays I'd go out with him fishing. In the winter the shad, they had a lot of good roe into them, I'd take and bust them and get a bucket of roe out of them and take it home.

"When I was thirteen I was mess-cooking at the factory for sixty-five men, two dollars a week. That was down in Southport. That's thirty miles below Wilmington, on the mouth of the Cape Fear River. My father was captain of a menhaden boat, and they moved the factory from Portsmouth down to Southport. That was a lot of money. You went to the movies – silent, they didn't have no talkies then – Friday nights, ten cent movies, get you a bag of peanuts for a nickel. Only sound in the movie house would be the poppin' of them peanuts. In World War One we moved to Beaufort, fishing that menhaden boat. When the war ended in 1918 I was in school there.

"When I come to be fourteen my father turned the boat over to me. I had a two-cylinder Lathrop in to her. Straight drive, you didn't have clutches then. You had to learn how to handle that switch. You had to know how to judge the wind and the distance comin' in. One time when we were going up the sound when I was sixteen she kicked back and smashed that finger there. So I still got a mark from that engine. I hauled cars across to Ocracoke with that boat. Down the shore side there I got two skiffs and I put 'em side by side and put planks on 'em. Then I'd put the cars on 'em and tow 'em across. Got ten dollars a car. See, boys were workin' away from home, Philadelphia and them, and they'd come home want to show their car off. Didn't have a road, but just flatten your tire down fourteen or fifteen pounds you could ride in the sand. Catch low water and you could ride the surf line. I've gone from here to Oregon Inlet in an hour. Course you didn't have traffic then.

"I used to have to hunt when I was a teenager. They had a private club there my father took care of. That's a unpleasant job, working for rich people. It was on the Sound, up on the Reef about four miles from here. In about six feet of water. We had blinds up on the reef and we had about 65 geese there in the yard. We were guides. They come down to go hunting, we – we had to go put the decoys out. We had metal pegs you tied their foot to it. Used about fifteen to eighteen to a battery. Live geese. See, they outlawed that.

"I think the hardest work I ever done was pushing a clam-rake. You only got fifteen cents a hundred for 'em in the thirties. That's hard work, worse'n any. You'd get three and four hundred clams a day. And you get you a can of sardines for a nickel, a coca-cola for a nickel, some crackers, well you had to catch a hundred clams to pay for your lunch. And pound netting for my father, that was hard work. And fishing in the ocean, and we pulled our nets by hand. They don't do that no more. Those nets out in the equipment house my mother and I knotted in the thirties. It all used to be cotton, linen. We used to buy the twine and tie them. We'd make our wooden gages the size we want the net. You don't tie too many yards in a night...we used to haul eleven hundred yards of net, get on the stern and pull them in by hand. About the second week of that you'd be gettin' in good shape. That's the way we used to work. But everything's push a button now.

"My father started going to sea when he was fourteen years old. His name was Charlie. He got eight dollars a month. He worked his way up to mate. He was on a three, four-mast schooner, I don't remember the name. He used to sail down to the West Indies, all that way.

"Ain't too much I know about my mother. She was born here in the woods and she never liked to go places. We lived in Beaufort for two years and then we come home. We were coming out of Beaufort Inlet and she told my father, this is my last trip to sea. Over the years she never had any use for the water. I had my first boat and she wouldn't never go to the dock to look at it. It didn't mean a thing to her. She was a Ballance. Her family was mostly fishermen, that was all there was here. They practically owned this beach down below the ferry dock. They just let it go; it wa'n't worth nothing. There was a local man here in the twenties taking it up for taxes and he sold it to some Yankees. And they had a fence across it all the way to the ocean, which was wrong. So I pried into that. A good friend of mine, the governor of North Carolina, said they'd back me in a test case. Some of them got mad at me over that. Then when the Park Service came along in the fifties they was first to sell, cause they knew they'd lost their rights. Park Service, best thing that ever happened to this island.

"I started the sport fishing out of here in '38. And the first summer I went it was a hundred dollars for four day trips out to the Gulf Stream. Twenty-five dollars a day was money then.

"What made me get into fishing? I just wanted to. I left home to keep from fishing. I went to New York, went two years in the Coast Guard in rum-running days. Then I worked in a sheet metal shop out in Long Island. It was pretty work, I spent five years putting copper roofs on them big summer homes. Then in '33, after the election, money people just closed up. And you can't live up there without work. So I came home. That depression running me home was the best thing ever happened to me. I lost the boat we had in '35, out on Diamond Shoals, my brother did. So then I built the *Albatross*. In '37.

"I got my lumber. It grows on the swamp, over on our mainland. Other people calls it white cedar, but we call it juniper. Cost me 4 1/2 cents a foot and the framing three cents a foot. I carried it down to Marshallburg and a man there built my boat. When I got her home she cost me eight hundred and five dollars. Without a engine. I went to the bank and borrowed seventy-five dollars, put a shaft in her. And I bought a Buick for fifteen dollars. Man said, drive it home, ain't nothing wrong with it. I said, don't want the car, just want the engine! Local man, Lloyd Styron here, he put her in for me. He said, Pay me when you make it. I borrowed a propeller. I borrowed a steering wheel. I borrowed a gas tank. That's how I started out in the *Albatross*. A lot of people don't believe a lot of this, but that's just the way it happened.

"It didn't take too long to pay that $75 back. Man at the bank said Ernal, just let that ride. I said no, I want that note! Because it was on my boat.

"So we went along. Later on I got a Chrysler engine, Airflow, straight eight, '34 model. But I got it hot and busted it. Then Burris, who owned the Texaco station, said, Ernal, I'll get you a engine. Six hundred dollars, a Chris Craft. So I went to the bank and borrowed it. This was in thirty-eight. That was some engine. We went along. Money was scarce. We were getting half a cent a pound for croaker, three cent for trout. I got that note paid off in December of 1941. And the second week after I got her paid off I got my notice from the Army.

"Draft! That killed me. I had a row with the girl in the office. I said, I'm thirty-two years old. I'm living, taking care of my father and mother. How can I support them on $21 a month? She said, that's your problem. She give me two weeks to think it over. Lloyd and I was the two oldest, he was thirty-seven, but we was drafted first! There was some paid off, so they wouldn't go. Think so? I know so.

"So I went to Norfolk, got in the Coast Guard. The Hooligan Navy. I knew I would, I'd been fishing for a year with this commander. I went in as a first class petty officer. Eighty-four dollars a month. I married Hazel here in '42. She's one of those Midgetts, they say the first one washed ashore in a whiskey barrel. Her grandfather you might have heard of, he saved a lot of people.

"I never been across the Atlantic. My brothers did, they were in the Navy. I was one of the lucky ones, I was here for four years. Baltimore was the farthest I got away from home.

"I was on a boat – harbor duty, sabotage, patrolling. We used to patrol the pierheads and Newport News, and the bridgehead. One merchant ship there come in with blood comin' out of the scupper holes. Had a mutiny on it. And when they paid off ships I stood guard. They paid off in cash, men come in one door of the mess hall and out the other. Wouldn't let but one man in at a time. I didn't like being guard – a gun's something I never had any use for. I got me a shotgun back there I bought in 1929 and I never had any use for it.

"Then for eighteen months I was on a patrol boat out of Morehead when they was sinking of these ships out here. It was bad. I didn't sleep when we were out on patrol – I was afraid one of those subs would blow us out of the water. This was a old 75-foot chaser they built to chase the rum-runners. We had a one-pounder on the bow and a fifty-caliber machine gun. I could throw a shell about as far as that one-pounder would shoot. We carried four depth charges. You dropped one of those, it was full speed ahead or it would knock the caulking out of your hull and you had to head for the shipyard.

"During that war you couldn't even rest here at night. It would jar you off your bed, almost knock the lights out and shake your windows. The concussion. You'd look out and see two or three ships burning at one time. I've fished over a lot of em. My son says oil's still flowing out of one of them.

"And then they took my boat! I get so mad about that I don't like to talk about her. They had her down there in Fort

Macon and painted her gray. They used her for a play toy.

"I had a time getting her back. I had a big row in the captain's office. 'You've been paid for that boat,' he said. I said, 'Show me where it's paid for.' I knew it hadn't because when they sent me the papers I put them in the stove and they went up the chimney. So he said, 'Well then we got a boat for nothing.' We had it out but when I was leaving I said, 'Captain, there's bigger men than you are.' He figured I was just a sailor. But I wrote to my congressman. I knew him since I was a boy. And I wrote a lawyer in Washington DC, which his father was some of my mother's people. And about two weeks I was called back in the office, and the captain invited me to sit down. And he wanted to help me get my boat back then.

"It was in bad shape. Painted gray inside and out, and they had burned the engine and clutch up. But I accepted it as it was. I wanted her back.

"I got back in forty-six. I'd had some lung trouble, spent six months in the hospital. Later on they found a growth in my lung. Took part of it out, some of my ribs. Doctor told me I couldn't work no more in the winter. So I figured then I'd just stick to my charter fishing. Didn't anybody else want to, they'd leave them on the dock to go shrimping. So I turned around, and instead of building a home I built the second boat, in '48. I had a little disability, but they cut that off in '52. So then instead of building a house we built the third boat. Then in '55 we finally had to tear down the old house, and I built this one. And we finally got it so we can live in it.

"Then my son Ernie was getting up in age, and we wanted

him to go to school. So we saved. We cut a lot of corners. No automobile, nothing. We could have asked for a handout from the government, but we didn't. My father always told me the government owes you nothing. You got to make your own way. And I never got on that social security till I was sixty-eight, cause I was working. Ernie's a schoolteacher up in Manteo now, and he comes down here summers. After I had the heart trouble I turned the boats over to him.

"But I got into this charter business, and just liked it. It was something different every day. At first we fished wrecks. Then we fished billfish. Out in the blue water you don't know what you're going to catch. It does something to you. When you see the fish come out'n the water walkin' on their tails. The more you do it the more you get encouraged. And it made you feel good to catch a fish.

"I used to have some nice customers. I've fished governors, ambassadors, senators. Ray Trallenger, from the New York World. Senator Duff. I used to have a bunch of girls too. One of them got sick on me out catching bluefish. She was redheaded. Blondes, lightheaded people get sick easier than darkheaded. All over I used to have coming in here. Those days it was a week or ten days at a time, man and his wife. If you didn't catch a fish, well, you'd catch one tomorrow. It's not like that any more. It's groups, five and six, and if they don't catch a boatload of fish they're mad.

"The most beautiful thing I ever saw at sea was a school of marlin. I thought at first it was porpoises. It was in the small tuna season. And they were knocking them in the air, then they'd jump. And there might be ten or fifteen of them in the air at the same time. And the sun was shining, and the water run off their back. A person hasn't seen it can't imagine it. It's blue and changes. And when they went into the air the sun would shine on them, the water running off almost like a blue rainbow. It's the only time I ever seen that.

"We don't have them out there like they used to. Used to be you'd hook two or three at a time. Big marlin. They're being overfished.

"The man who wrote this book about the Albatross Fleet, John Cleveland, he was the first one to release a marlin. He started fishing with me in '58. And he made me release the biggest sailfish ever been caught on this coast. I imagine he was ten feet long. They live after they're released, if they're not bleeding. Sometimes I just cut the wire, but if I can I sit on the stern and shake the hooks out of 'em. I don't like to kill fish if you're not goin' to use them.

"These tournaments are just disgusting. A bunch of millionaires had this tournament, up at this club. And they lie, steal, cheat...it's sad. Instead of having a fun tournament money got involved, and they'll do anything to win. Used to be they'd release them. Then once one of those yachts was fishing close to my boat and he lost the fish, a hundred yards back when he jumped off. And he called in that he released a fish! Now they have to bring them in, they stopped trusting each other. But there's all a new group there at that club now. I walk up there at night and I don't know anybody. Some of them there now got a glass in each hand and one in their mouth. To drown their problems. They're not happy people.

"Fishing is going to go up and down. But now there's

laws, and limits. That's federal. State don't mess with it. But I don't like that. And now I got to pay tax on my boats, same as a commercial fisherman. Another thing I don't like is people selling their fish off my boat. If they don't want to take them home and eat it themselves, I say release it. But there's more people fishing now. Used to be I was out for five, six days and I was the only boat out there.

"I never used charts. Or compass. I never used Loran. I carried a boat to New York with no chart. Every place on the coast is in my mind just like you're on a highway. I know how much time I make and I just go where I want to go. I can't tell anybody the courses, but it just comes to me. My family is all natural born watermen. Now they got depth recorders. *Colored* depth recorders! They got *temperature* gauges! I used to use my finger.

"You know, I think if the people today had to live like we had to live they'd see it differently. Young people today, all they think is money. They get sixteen, they got to have them a car! You got to have money to live, but if you get to craving it you can forget living. I never worried to pile up a lot of it. I wouldn't be doing anything different if I was rich. I done what I set out to do and I'm happy.

"I look back over the years and how I had to struggle. And in a way I still ain't got nothing. But I got Hazel, home, children, we got a lot to be thankful for. Two years ago I had a heart problem, they told me I couldn't go to the dock no more. I guess I let little things get to me too much. When the boat broke down, things like that. Had to give up everything! But I haven't. I invited those doctors down in August and took them out fishing.

"I still mess with the boats every day, piddle around. But now I try not to let things bother me. I sit on the dock and whittle. Don't make nothing but a mess. And I wait for my boats and my boys to come back in."

A LIFE IN MANTEO:
Benjamin Allen Creef

Well, I was born in 1918. I was the first child of my mother and father's second marriage. My father's first wife died; and my mother's first husband died. My mother's maiden name was Chappell.

"The Chapells were a Perquimans County family, and they moved to Elizabeth City when she was just a child, I've been told. And my mother's first husband was a Bliven. They were an older family here on Roanoke Island. She was in Elizabeth City when she met her first husband.

"My father's family has been on the island for a long time. They say Creefs come here sometime in the 17s. We think on the Creef side they were from the section between Germany and France called Alsace-Lorraine. They say the name appears there on some village. But also in Currituck County, the name Moncrief is there, and without any explanation at all here is the same Thomas and William, but it's no longer Moncrief, but Creef.

"My grandfather I think was born in East Lake; and then he came over here, and he built the shad boats that were the smart little boats out here in the sounds back before the turn of the century. And he was credited with being the first to build one. Now, Captain Balfour Baum would stand against that if he was still alive. Balfour – that's an old name. His daddy was Judge Baum here in Manteo. Balfour said he had always heard it said that Mr. Barnett was the one who built the first shad boat and my daddy copied it. Well, daddy was a copier. He had an older man come through here going to Florida and he left a small speedboat made of some heavier wood, and when he came back through my half brother and daddy challenged him to a race. What they had done was, they copied her and made her out of the light juniper, and she beat his boat. It was just more or less a thing they were always doing. Living here on this little isolated island back in those days I imagine they could do anything they wanted, without too much interference.

"They went out in the woods and got the knees, not straight pieces, and formed the inside part of the boat; then planked her, with juniper. The odd thing about it is, for two generations ahead of me they all went into boatbuilding. It was my own father's boat that carried the Wright Brothers across from Elizabeth City to Kitty Hawk. The *Hattie Creef*. It was built as a three master. It was a sailboat to start with; it was used commercially, for hauling fish, mostly, in its later years. It went out of Wanchese and if it had a signal it made a port call to Manns Harbor on its way up the sound, the Croatan, and then went on to Elizabeth City. And usually it was a early morning rise and leave, and if you wanted to come back on the same day you'd have to rush back down to the dock in Elizabeth City to get back on. My father built that boat on the shore, just south of Fort Raleigh. That's what I've always been told; but then there was an old fellow that lived in Skyco and he said to me, 'Oh, I remember comin' to Manteo when they launched her.' So I think she must have been built on the railway here. But she could have been built on skids. We had one big one called the *Standard* that was built for Muncie Daniels here, the Esso dealer. She was built on skids up here. And for years after it was sunk, here in the harbor in Manteo, an old man from up in Camden County lived in the cabin, which was above water. Yes, daddy built boats. George Washington the IInd built boats. My grandfather was George Washington Creef the First.

"The boats that I remember them building were built along a railway along the waterfront here in Manteo, close to where the Elizabeth II was built. I was never very much help. All of those older fellows, back in those days, were like a lot of old folks today – get out of my sight, get out of my way, this that and the other. We had to respect our older – well, my daddy and his brother run the boat yard, and at noon time they went up in the loft of the building and we were told either to get away or keep quiet; so it was easier to get away. They just took a little siesta in the middle of the day. They would eat their breakfast at a little restaurant on the waterfront before daybreak, and turn to work and then in the middle of the day they'd take their siesta. Knock off at nightfall – though sometimes in the winter they'd work maybe a little later, and come home then. But in the summertime they would knock off fairly early. Oh, we didn't have very dependable power plant until sometime in the twenties or early thirties. See, when I was real small we had our own light plant, we had our own phone company, we had our own bank, we had our own dairy. And I remember seein' them ship May peas out of here in hampers to the market. Now they come in in a can, or frozen.

"My dad's other love was the theater, and he had the motion picture theater in the town of Manteo the year that I was born. I was born in January, and my mother and father opened the theatre the same year, in November. That was the first theater around here. It was named the Pioneer, and still has the Pioneer name. On the corner where the city hall is now there was an old academy. They moved that building down to the waterfront. That was my mother's money and my father's ingenuity that put that theater up. In those early years my half brother, Herbert Creef, operated the show. And he had Lee Hassell and other fellows operatin' the machine. My brother reasoned that as long as he had that theater in that building that was my mother's and the rest of the family's belongings. But in 1934 we moved the theater down to Budleigh, closed on March 17 and opened up the next day in the new buildin' without losin' a show. But then that was his theater. My mother just handed it over to him.

"My brother's – now this is the things that my wife sort of hates for me to say, but my half-brother. His mother was the lady that died on my father's first go-around. Sometimes you're just a plain outcast in certain situations. I told somebody once when I was old enough to realize that this really didn't worry me, that I must have been a pretty unpopular guy when I first came on this earth, to think that I had a sister older than my mother.

"Well, in the early twenties. . . we had it fairly easy here in comparison to some places, it seems to me. Of course my daddy died when I was ten, and this sort of put a strain on Mother; and of course I wasn't old enough to know very much what to do or how to do anything. But I started working at the theater when I was twelve or thirteen years of age.

"No, I couldn't run the machines at that age. But I went down to the boat and got the films off the boat. You see, nothin' came overland. Back in the twenties. The *Hattie Creef* boat was in Wanchese in my time, but before that the steamer *Neuse* came in in Skyco. An old black lady was talking to me 'bout a year, year and a half ago about traveling on the steamer *Neuse*. Miss Mossie; she's dead now. She was a maid in Guy Lombardo's home in New York.

"When I was real small, during the day I would go in and sweep. And at night, in the time when our pictures were still silent, I would sell candy bars between reels. I believe the Milky Way was there at that time. And I would take peanuts from the jar – I believe they called them confectionary jars. I would go and buy the peanuts and had what they called glassine bags – not cellophane, it was sort of an oily bag, and put the peanuts in them and sell them between reels.

"When I was a boy I had it pretty tough. After my daddy died, my half-brother – I've always been grateful for the fact that he was around because he just more or less stepped in, and was my daddy from then on. He was as much as sixteen or seventeen years older. When I was real small he was in the same house with us, but when I was old enough to know very much he had already built another home. He and his wife.

"Herbert Blivens' daddy lived in the home with me. And my mother. So I had two half brothers. To make it stranger, I had two half brothers named Herbert Creef. Herbert Creef Blivens, and Herbert Augustus Creef. My mother's first husband was very close to the Creefs. So when Herbert Blivens was born they named him Herbert Creef Blivens. I had two half sisters, Hattie Creef and Ella Creef. She is the one that the boat was named for.

"When I was small we played marbles, and I was always around the waterfront with a dip-net in season, catchin' crabs and catchin' fish off the end of the little piers that we had at that time. You could walk, in Manteo, from where the bridge is now going to Ice Plant Island, around to where the Elizabeth II was built – well, you could walk from one boat, to a dock, to another boat, to a dock, all the way across that waterfront. Everyone had a boat then, because there wasn't but four or five cars here on the island.

"I wasn't really good at sports. In the baseball, I would visit my half-sister and her children, who were about my age, in Norfolk. And playing sandlot ball, just for kicks they would get me to play with them. And they'd throw me a curve. And the durn thing would hit me somewheres, instead of in the glove. Well, I have a real funny story I can tell you on that. I was real clumsy. I couldn't hit the ball, I couldn't catch it, and so in my high school days I went out for baseball. And the guys were all hangin' around the edge of the field, and they called me over and says, 'Will you be manager?' So that was the end of my baseball career. I just wasn't – wasn't any good at it. Now one or two of my nephews were good in baseball years later.

"What was I good at? I was in the first basketball team to win the state tournament. Manteo High School, 1936. But I wasn't a star. I played center. That was when we had a tipoff after every point. That slowed it down a whole lot. Wasn't anything unusual to have a game 12 or 18 points. We played outdoors, we didn't have any inside gyms at that time, and played on dirt courts. I still follow that basketball pretty close.

"I graduated in '36. And I worked at the theater primarily. And let's see now. Thirty-six was the year the Lost Colony started. And like a lot of other young fellows around here, it gave us an opportunity to work at a few more things than the other places had at the time. The Depression was still pretty tight and I worked a few hours a day at a service station, a few hours a day at a drug store, and I worked at night at the theater.

"I didn't start runnin' the machines alone till I was 16. We had what was called a Powers. But we later put in the Century. The Century was an update machine at that time. Well, when I first started being around the machines they were hand-cranked. I do remember seeing my brother crank the machines. Yes, we had a piano player. The better shows that come in would have the big sheet music with the show. They certainly put the mood in. If it was a villain you'd have your villain music, or if it was something light you'd have light music. Our piano player was Miss Naomi Wescott. She was Mrs. Eber Wescott. And I remember one hot day that I went down to set up the light for her piano, and was workin' on puttin' a fan so she could get some little bit cooler air – it was a hot day and of course we didn't have no air conditioning that time – and I put the plug in the open bulb socket and got a little bit of a spark. It was just a childlike error on my part. Course I wasn't a child at that time, should of known better.

"I remember 'The Sin of Madame Claudette' – and then I remember 'King of Kings' – and oh, 'Over the Hill's the Poorhouse'. That was sound on record. The film was synchronized with the turntable. It was hard to do, especially when you had a break in the film or a bad groove in the record. I remember in this 'Over the Hill's the Poorhouse' it got out of sync, and this old lady was downstairs in this particular scene, and she was hollerin' to somebody upstairs, and the scene had already shifted to outdoors and the old lady was still sayin' 'Get up. . . get up. . . get up. . . .' The record had stuck. Of all the people that I remember growing up that Claudette Colbert was one of my favorites. And I sort of liked Marlene Dietrich. I met her in Greenland. She came in and sat down on my bunk and talked to us for a while. She was a big star even then. She was quite a nice person.

"I have to say that was the roughest time I've had, was finishing high school and trying to work at the same time. And bein' without a father.

"I had an opportunity when I was just out of high school, I could have gone to the distributors, the headquarters. We entertained the owners and salesmen – they were a bigger deal than they are this day and time. And they – anyway, we used to entertain them on boats like Ernal Foster's boat, and they'd take them out deep-sea fishing and this that and the other; and while I was reserved to run the theater at night, I met them when they were in town over a meal or a soda at their hotel lobby or something, and they – this was after we had the 2000-foot reels and we had some time to stand around and talk to them in the booth. And I could tell them things about the shows that were comin' out and this that and the other and they would say, 'Gee whiz, you know more about this than I do.' And I would say, after all I have this time to read about this stuff while I'm runnin' this twenty-minute reels and – I got pretty well filled in with a lot of things.

"I could have followed through on that with the distributor easily. I just never give any thought to leaving Manteo. This was before I was ever married the first time. I was more or less married to that projection booth.

"I was able to get in the Coast Guard, in 1942, when I was twenty-four. The Army was breathin' down my back. My brother wanted me to stay close to home and he thought if I could get in the Coast Guard I could get home. So this is what really happened. I signed in in Norfolk Virginia and I guess you would say was lucky enough to get transferred down to Elizabeth City. I stayed there for a year and a half. And I got so tired of being called a 'home guard' that I volunteered for overseas. And sure enough they let me go.

"I went to aerial gunnery school at Dam Neck, Virginia. I found out while I was at Dam Neck that the main part of the training was for PBM service in the South Pacific. I just didn't act as a coward along that line, but I figured that I'd rather be in the North Atlantic than the South Pacific. And so when I came back to the base after my aerial gunnery training, in

1944, that's where I went.

"You see, the Coast Guard had the reputation of already being used to those conditions – of the icebergs, and the cold, and all. Admiral 'Iceberg' Smith was our commandin' officer, and he was over the Navy and the Army in the North Atlantic. His headquarters were in Argentia Newfoundland, Navy 103.

"We did what they called Dumbo – the air-sea rescue. We covered for ships at sea. One of the things that we did quite often, was whenever a carrier would have a covey of planes take off on practice or somethin', we would get above 'em and lead 'em back into their base. The weather was real tough up there and we did a lot of that kind of stuff. This was the PBY-5A, which has the two engines and the landing gear. I learned to love the thing. It was a slow baby but I had some good hours in it. I was a mechanic.

"In Greenland it was real slow. I've boasted that I've flown sunup to sundown, day in and day out. But up there sunup to sundown is only four hours. I was at Bluey West One, which is on the west coast, somewhat south of the Arctic Circle. Did I see any Germans? Only captured. They were being marshalled, marched from one place to another.

"I mustered out in November, I believe, of '45. 11/21/45. This is my mustering-out card here. Still carry it. The officer that gave us that gave us one of the little Ruptured Duck pins too. And he said, 'Remember now, anywhere you go in the United States, one of these and five cents and you can get a cup of coffee.'

"I came back and went to work for the theater.

"I had a broken marriage when I was overseas. My first

wife had found someone she thought more of than she thought of me. So I went ahead and got a divorce. I got married first in '42. Wanchese girl. I think it was a matter of her being so young. Oh, incidentally, she's been dead for a number of years now. . . she married a second time. And she got religion and left him and after they'd been separated a good while he died of cancer in the same year that she got religion. This seems to be the way that sometimes when some people go to holiness they change their whole livelihood of life the way that things of this sort are concerned. She felt like then that she'd been living in sin, she'd had two husbands and all this that and the other. There was never any makeup with me; I never attempted to be seen or see her again after the divorce was final, that was really. . . .well, I was hurt. And I think that it was more pride than anything else. And then when I realized she didn't care anything for me there wasn't any need for me holding out any hopes. I didn't think I'd ever marry again when it first happened. Men have something going and women have something going too. We're having a bad situation now, my oldest daughter is thirty-nine I believe, and her husband proved to be unfaithful. She's gettin' her separation papers and they're all being signed this weekend. They have a ten-year-old child.

"And then when I got out of service in '45 I came back home. And then I met my present wife in '47, I think it was. My second wife's brother was the former representative, Stanford White. Her name is Louise. We were married in '47. We courted here. The ferry was still runnin' between Manns Harbor and Manteo and during our courtin' time she worked in Manteo. But I usually worked the machines in the theater at night. And it sort of made for a late date. But a lot of times I would ride over to Manns Harbor on the ferry after I got off work. And then when it got to be a serious situation to us, then she didn't want to get married in Manns Harbor, and she didn't think it was proper for us to get married to Manteo. We was both Methodists. And so my half sister who lived in Norfolk found that out so she made arrangements for us to get married in Norfolk. At Park Place Methodist Church.

"I think that the first marriage had sort of put a damper on the idea of even gettin' married here. See, I had the girl gave me the ring back. I had all the china and silverware that my family had given on the first marriage. And when we decided to get married I brought up the fact of the ring and the china and Louise said, 'Well, I can use that.' Wasn't anything wrong with the idea; 'It was your people who gave it.' So then I said what about the stone, and she said, 'Well, if you want to put it on another ring.' And so I traded that ring in on the. . . present ring. I got the stone in Elizabeth City, at Lewis Selig's. I don't remember what carat it was. It wasn't so very big, but it was bigger than a lot of people have.

"I was still at the theater then. I worked there about forty years.

"After the war I went to the Navy Yard in Norfolk. Since I had done aviation work during the war I went up there after Louise and I were first married, to get a job on the air station. I also went to the Ford plant, and almost got hired, but the foreman up there checked my hand, did everything but ask me. I think he was interested in me, I could have done the work there on the line. And another fellow who worked there I talked to him, and told him about the turn-down, and he said, 'Of course, you wasn't a Mason.'

"One of the jobs I had after Louise and I were married, I drove the mail down to Hatteras and back. And that company sold out to a bus company in Elizabeth City, and they offered me the job driving a bus down there. And I said, 'I'm thirty years old, and I never drove a bus, and I'm not goin' to start now.' But later on I did drive a mail truck, and I drove through three hurricanes down here. And the third one I went through, it must have been '54, there wasn't any road – the ocean tide had cut it out. At the bad spots I gave the wheel to a man from Hatteras who was ridin' with me. He knew them better than I would. It was really rough. I ended that day taking the first class bags out and bummin' a ride into Hatteras Village on a four-wheel drive.

"It was after that hurricane that I went to work for the Park Service. I worked for them twenty one years, truck driver and warehouseman at Bodie Island. And showed movies at night. Yep, my family got cheated. And my theater job wasn't a paying job. My brother never paid me what it was worth.

"The time I enjoyed the most? I think when I was about forty years old. I had learned enough about life to see that it had – well, at 40 my present wife and I had been married about ten years. If you want to put it down in book form, those were about the best years. When the three children were small. One daughter and two sons. Those were the most pleasant years of my life.

"The old two-story frame house almost directly in front of

the fire station is where I lived a good part of that time. Where I grew up. It was twenty-five years ago we got the new home. We have deeded the older house over to our youngest son. And he's hopin' to get a roof on it.

"The two boys are both carpenters. The younger one is a more settled person and has been in the industry longer than the older one. The woodworking runs in the family – sort of rubbed off. The youngest boy lives in the barn back of the two-story house. He built the barn. It's a nice unit. The older one lives in a trailer up the north end of the island. My daughter is in the school system down in Clinton, a sort of a vocation placement job.

"I've been pretty happy living in Manteo. I grew up around here with all these people and consider most of them my friends. I don't believe I have any political enemies, or otherwise enemies.

"I think Manteo has changed a lot in the last sixty years. Just in terms of the transportation. When I was a little boy the steamer *Trenton* came in, it was running between Manteo and Elizabeth City years before they put the *Hattie Creef* on for the same run. After they had the wooden rickety bridges – they wasn't rickety when they was built, but it didn't take them long to get that way – we had business people here in Manteo that when that opened this area up to automobile transportation they just went out of their business. They were smart enough to know they couldn't compete. For wholesale groceries and the like.

"Yes, the people have changed too. There are a lot of blue-eyed people here. Predominantly; and years ago, when everybody I knew was somebody I knew, or I knew their people, they were all blond. They say that the people who lived in Stumpy Point and the people who lived in Buxton, all the same name – relatives. Over all that expanse of water, it was the closest way for them to go, because of the wind.

"I think we still got some people who were greedy then and their grandchildren are greedy now. Anxious to get their hands on monies and what have you. We have people here who like to make that dollar. I myself was pretty happy to just be a family man. I haven't had the ambition some have had, and I haven't had the disappointments some have had.

"If I had my life to live over again, though, I'd of bought a bunch of beach property. It was available to any of us at that time. We just didn't have the foresight. My half brother, who's worth more than I'll ever be, never had any faith in anything over't that beach. Because it won't take but one hurricane to wipe you out.

"I'm pretty happy now. Satisfied. And grateful. You know, some of the people who are dead and gone worked themselves to death. I don't intend to. All in all, I try to have a good outlook on life. I try to spend my time trying to help someone else, 'stead of tryin' to help myself. I go to the nutrition site five days a week most every week, and there is a lot of people there that are not as well off as I am financially...or physically...or mentally. And we have one blind person who when I am there I'm the one cuts his food up. And there's people there who want postage stamps, or a letter mailed, or get a check cashed for 'em or something of this sort, and usually I'm the one that goes and does that. And some of the older people will see me do things like that, and they say, 'You shouldn't do that.' And I just thank God I can.

"See, I had an experience nine years ago. I was workin' for the Park Service and working at the theater at the same time – what they call moonlighting. And I had a stroke, which sort of set me back. I was in the hospital in Elizabeth City for nine days. And then they sent me to Norfolk. The doctor said it was a Christmas stroke – it was kind to me. And for a while there I wasn't able to think or act like myself. But I worked my way back. But I was forced to – well, not forced, but it was the best thing for me to just withdraw from the government job I had.

"I have been real active in Lions Club for a few years. In the last nine years I have been named Lion of the Year twice. I sell a lot of the brooms, the calendars. I like to stay in the yard as much as I can. I rake up the pecans I don't use, because they're not full, some of the trees don't give a full nut – I rake these up and rather than throw them away I take them out to the colored section and give them a big bag of them. Somebody that doesn't have anything at all they appreciate them."

CURIOSITY LANE:
Elizabeth Ann O'Neal Howard

The house is small and white behind its picket fence and its two live oaks. The lane is so small it has no name. "But we call it Curiosity Lane," says Elizabeth Howard, laughing like a mischievous thirteen-year-old. "Because everybody who lives here is so curious. Come on in! Let's sit in the living room. I talk better from my chair."

"I was born in nineteen ten, in what we call the Trent Woods. It was beautiful up there. I wish I could take you up and show you. There wasn't a many of houses; we all lived in that one little neighborhood; there were three houses, and then one farther down, and then that was all. It's up on the Bay. I better not say what the name of that bay used to be...when I was born there were six of us, me and my two brothers and my father and mother, and then there were my cousins.

"My daddy when he was young, he went to sea. He was born up in Trent too. There was forty-seven acres and there was my grandmother, my uncle and aunt, and my father and mother. And my uncle and my father each had three children, so there were six of us. My mother had four children, but my oldest brother died. He saw a duck, and he shot the duck, and he went in to get it. And it was freezing cold, and he caught pneumonia and died four years before I was born. Doctor MacIntyre gave him medicine but it didn't pull him through.

"I can go back in my family to seventeen hundred and fifty-nine. William Howard came and bought the island in 1759. And with him came John Williams, who was a pilot. And he witnessed the deeds. Then two months later John Williams came back and bought half of the island from William Howard. I married a Howard; but I'm an O'Neal. And my mother was a Williams. So I am about...fifth generation from John Williams.

"The O'Neal that I came from, I can't go back farther than 1774 on the O'Neal side. That's when Elizabeth Jackson married John O'Neal. And they had ten children. And I came from Christopher O'Neal, who was the youngest boy.

"My grandfather Horatio Williams was an old sea captain. My mother and her sister sailed to New York City on his vessel, the *Paragon*. And he gave them money and told them to go ashore and buy whatever they wanted. My mother's sister bought a bedroom suit, and my mother bought cashmere and embroidery and ribbons and things. For her trousseau. There were three men on the vessel, and he sent them ashore to look after them. But they all three got drunk and she and her sister had to get back to the boat the best way they could.

"When I was two and a half years old, my father bought the house that's around the corner. And they moved down here to the creek side of the island. Then later my father bought the store on the Lake. My daddy was then in the Lifesaving Service, so my double-cousin and my brother operated the store. So I've lived in this neighborhood seventy-three and a half years.

"When I was a little girl we played bob-jacks, little things made out of metal and you throw the jack up and catch them. We didn't use a ball. And we played what we called hop scotch, and croquet, and dolls. I had a lot of books with paper dolls in them; and we also cut the pictures out of the catalog and played with them.

"We had what you call a Hot Blast – a big stove that would hold wood and coal. In our living room we had a two-burner stove that looked like a piece of furniture. Kerosene. And then the kind you carry around in your hand, we had those in the bedrooms. And a fireplace in the living room, but I never used that when I was young, and now I'm old I still don't. In the kitchen we had a big iron stove with a reservoir to keep the water hot. That burned wood.

"In the summer my mother would cook on the oil stove to keep the kitchen from getting hot. In the winter she would use the wood stove. For breakfast we would have ham and eggs, or hot rolls homemade; or you could have oatmeal; or grits; or fish if you liked. I never liked fish for breakfast, I didn't like the smell. We had our main meal, what we called dinner and is now called lunch, in the middle of the day. Because when you don't have 'lectric, dark especially in the wintertime comes early. That's an old kerosene lamp there that belonged to my mother. For dinner we had chicken, it could be baked or stewed; we had lamb, my daddy had sheep on the Banks. We had oysters, fish, crab, clams, wild duck, hog meat. The hogs lived in pens in people's yards. My father had cattle down below and every week he would kill a heifer and sell it in the store. He had a refrigerator in the store that would hold sixteen cakes of ice, and twice a week he would get ice and have a man cut the meat up and he would sell it. The sheep lived on the banks, from where the pony pen is now to the town. They just roamed free. My daddy's branding iron was a diamond shape. My daddy would buy the stock and the feed and my uncle would do the work.

"Our water came from cisterns. And some people had rain barrels. A cistern catches rain water from the roof. And a lot of people had wells and lift pumps. Well, honey, you had to bathe in a wash tub or a wash basin. I played in the dirt and I took a bath every day. You were never put to bed dirty, I can tell you that. The cleanest people on earth are right here on this island. And that still goes in our family.

"I saw my first airplane in 1916, 1917. I was six or seven. It was at a funeral, it was a family connection. People were standing around out in the yard and heard the roaring of the plane. And everybody fell on the ground. They were frightened, they didn't know what the plane was there for. It was World War One. Wouldn't you have been frightened?

"I don't know how old I was when I first went off the island. I took the mail boat. It was a bugeye. It took nine hours. It went out every day, except in the hurricane of '44. I got sea-sick. When I was a little girl I never wanted to travel around. Later on I wanted to but I never did. And now it's just too hard. I don't really want to any more.

"I could go anywhere I wanted on the island when I was a little girl. But I couldn't wear pants, my daddy wouldn't let me. I wear them now, but he never saw me in pants. I had pretty dresses. My mother had three boys, so she knew how to make boy clothes, but she wasn't too good at making girl clothes; so my aunts, my blood kin and my aunt by marriage, made all my dresses. I had three or four silk dresses, Sunday dresses, and maybe seven or eight cotton I wore the rest of the week. The Sunday dresses I would wear all day. And I remember the minister's son lived right across from us, and this little boy and I were playing, and we got in to some briars and I tore my silk dress. And my mother didn't spank me. She never spanked me for tearing my dresses. She only spanked me when I talked back to her.

"I wasn't allowed to go barefoot either. My daddy wouldn't let me go barefooted because we had horses in the yard. He was afraid of lockjaw. I wore Mary Janes, with straps, patent leather. But when my father wasn't home I used to go across the street with the parson's children and take my shoes off and play in the sand.

"At Christmas we would have a tree and Santa Claus would come. And everybody would go to the church, to the exercise on Christmas Eve. The Methodist church, that's all we had then. There would be a tree there too, and it's traditional that everybody who goes gets a bag of candy and peanuts, raisins, apple, orange in that bag. All of my life that happened, and I don't know how many years before. And on Christmas Eve night all the children had recitations, and we would put on a pageant. I can't remember anything I recited, but I remember one little boy, I can always remember the things I don't need to – he had a recitation that went, "Who's old Santy, I don't know/Great long whiskers hangin' down so." That little boy's name was Thomas Gilbert Jackson. He is still living here.

"You gave presents, you gave every member of your family presents. I remember when I believed in Santa Claus, that is I didn't know but what there wasn't a Santa Claus, I remember my cousin taking me to the other side of the Lake, to John McWilliam's store. She got a little toy cooking stove, and little frying pan, little pot, and then she bought a little clothesline and pins, and a big ball. Maybe I was a little stupid, but I didn't think anything about it. Oh, and a little tea set, and a little piano. And we left and I never thought about it and my mother hid everything for Christmas. But I searched, and I found it and I was in trouble. To this day I can never put anything back in a drawer the way I found it. But the next year the other children told me there wa'n't any Santa Claus. I don't know how I thought he got here – probably on the mail boat.

"What did we do in the winter? Some people quilted; I don't but I have some beautiful ones that were given to me. Do you know what a Chautaqua is? The Chautaqua came twice a year. And there were dances for the adults maybe every weekend, and in the summer every night. At the dance hall. One was down near the docks and the other was at the Pamlico Inn. And then there was one at the Odd Fellows' Lodge. When I grew up I danced at all of them. And people had parties in their homes. Dinner parties, and parties for the children. And candy-pulling, where you make candy and pull it and put it on a plate and let it get hard. And people would put on shows, they still do. Of course we had radios. But no one on the island knew how to fix them. So we just bought new ones when they wouldn't work any more.

"I grew up fast. All through my childhood I was taller than most children my age...when I was ten years old my father left the store in the neighborhood and moved down to the waterfront. My first cousin went with us and my mama sent me down there too. I had chores to do; I had to empty the Pepsi container, where they'd throw their empty bottles, and I had to take the trash out, sweep the front porch, and I had to take the oranges that were going bad out of the orange box, and the apples, and the grape box, had to throw away all the things you couldn't sell. The name of the store was Big Ike's. His name was Ike. It was on the waterfront. When I was a little girl the big boats couldn't get into the creek. The sailing vessels had to anchor out in the sound and you'd have to send a man out in his skiff and get my daddy's goods off the boat and bring it to my daddy's pier. You could pole out with a big oar.

"I was about twelve years old when a man from Hatteras came over here selling Model T Fords and my daddy bought one. And you know what he paid for it? Five hundred dollars. And Dallas Williams and David Williams bought one from the same man. Then later Captain Bill Gaskill bought a great big truck. He had the Pamlico Inn, that was where they took boarders – tourists. Tourists came here before I was ever born. This picture was taken in 1915 when I was five years old...this hotel had a hundred rooms. And I remember we were looking at that truck and somebody said, 'Captain Bill, is that a Ford?' And he said, 'It's all I can a-ford.'

"The cars could take you to the beach, but frankly you pushed more than you rode. If we left the island, going to

Hatteras, we rode the high-water mark. We'd have to leave the car down at the inlet and took the Coast Guard boat across. On the other side we'd visit among our relatives and come back the same way we went.

"During the depression there wasn't any money here. People who were in the Coast Guard, or the lighthouse, it didn't hurt them. But it hurt our family. It knocked the props from under my father. Because if you have a business and nobody has any money you can't sell anything, and if you do it just goes on the books...but even at that, nobody here went hungry. You couldn't here, you had fish, crabs, oysters were plentiful. That's what they'd give you at the store. Everybody had gardens.

"I finished the eighth grade here, then I went to school in North Carolina. Most children did that. I was fifteen when I went away to school. It was a private school which I thought was the army – you got up by the bugle and you went to bed with the bugle. It isn't there any more.

"After high school I wanted the bright lights and glitter, and the five and ten cent store. I had a job offered to me in Raleigh, to work with a doctor. I wrote to my mother telling her that and she wrote telling me to come home, my father needed me. So I came home. And I worked in my daddy's store. And after that I worked for Robert S. Wahab at what used to be the Wahab Hotel. They had the hotel, a skating rink, a movie theatre, and the dance hall, the Spanish Casino.

"That's another thing, why people came to Ocracoke and lived during the summer. Malaria, on the mainland. And you wouldn't get it on Ocracoke; these salt water mosquitoes don't carry malaria. All the little houses along the sound side were the people who came here during the summer to get away from the malaria.

"I married a Howard, Robert Wahab Howard. Did we grow up together...yes and no; I was three years older than he was and he grew up to me. That's a picture of him over there in his Navy uniform. He was a good-looking man, and he was smart. He was only in for the duration of the war but he made permanent chief. He could have stayed in. I wanted him to, but one day he took me aside and said, 'I got something to say and I want you to listen. If I stay in we won't have much time together. I want a home and a family, and I want to be home with my family. So don't tell me any more you want me to stay in the Navy.' I always thought he could have gotten the pension...but he died when he was only sixty. I thought then, he must have known. We were married in 1942. August the seventeenth.

"My daughter was born in the house around the corner from me. She wasn't supposed to be. I was supposed to be in Washington N.C., Little Washington the Tarheels call it. But she came early when I was getting dressed to get on the mail boat. I was making coffee when I felt the first pains. They brought a bed downstairs and that's where they put me. They had a registered nurse here and a practical nurse, Lola Williams, and they delivered my daughter. Lola stayed with me for ten days. And I remember my father said to my mother, 'Helen, that child will talk sooner than any child ever talked.' And my mother said, 'Why do you say that?' And my father said, 'Because she's been in that room with Lola and

Elizabeth for ten days and they haven't shut up once.'

"In World War Two things changed. You could go down to the naval base, if you had family in the Navy, and you could buy anything you wanted – a gold watch or anything. They had entertainment, USO shows. I never saw a ship actually get torpedoed; but we could hear it, boom boom booom. And you could step up on my daddy's porch and see the blaze. In that respect it was scary here. Everything was blacked out. The lighthouse had a blind on it. I asked my daddy one night, 'Papa, if the Germans take Ocracoke what will we do?' He said, 'Well honey I don't know what you'll do, but I think I'll kill m'self.' And my sister-in-law's a full-fledged German.

"Now things are changing here like everywhere. I don't think people here are as friendly as they used to be when I was growing up. People used to share their food. And we still do in this neighborhood, and I'm sure in the other neighborhoods too. But not everybody's like that. They can't afford to be. One thing, we don't have too many original families here any more. That's the Williamses, the O'Neals, the Garrishes, the Howards, and the Gaskills. And the Scarboroughs and the Spencers. They're all originally Ocracokers. Well, I won't say all the children are originals because their fathers or mothers may have come from some other place. I'm actually all Ocracoke. O'Neal and Williams and Tolson and Jackson. English and they say the Williamses are Welsh. Isn't it different where you live, where your grandmother lived, than it is now? I don't want to say things that will offend anybody, but when I grew up Ocracoke had the best class of people.

"The nicest thing about it still is that people here have more freedom. You don't live in fear here as much as in the cities. When my little girl was little she could run anywhere on the island, and in fact we'd let her take people around. Nothing has ever hurt me so I've never been afraid of things.

"My granddaughters now, for instance, they're nineteen and twenty-one. And they come and stay with me every summer. They wear pants. So that's changed. But I remember something my daddy said to my mother once, when I was fifteen and my cousin and I wanted to go to Hatteras for a dance, the Woodmen of the World opening, and stay overnight with our relatives. My mother said I shouldn't go, that her mother would never have allowed her to. But my father said, 'Let them go. Time changes. And people have to change with it.' I always remembered that because like it or not I think he was right.

"Would you like a cup of tea? Let's go in the kitchen. And we have some sweet potato pie, and someone brought over a bag of oysters this morning. Do you like vinegar on your oysters? I have some vinegar with peppers in it here I made...."

I MAY BECOME A CULTIVATED MAN:
Nicholas Longworth Meekins

The house is small, neat, one of dozens just like it in the tract in western Manteo.

Inside, wrapped in a vanilla-scented cloud of Captain Black that fills the living room, Nicholas Meekins is sitting back, repacking a curved briar pipe. He is a tall man with a pepper and salt moustache. He's still not entirely gray, but he finds it difficult to get up from his easy chair.

"When I was born? July twentieth, nineteen oh five.

"My father's name was Theodore Meekins. They have a plaque down there right where Pea Island Station was located. It mentions the fact that my father was on patrol that particular night when this *C. E. Newman* run aground. And he sounded the alarm and rushed to the station, and the crew got ready to go out and rescue the passengers.

"Now, I might be a little biased, but a neutral report, if it was given, would say that not only did my father sound the alarm, but – they have what they called a Lyle gun. They shoot this line across the bow of a ship. And they attach the breeches buoy and bring them ashore. Well, the Lyle gun wouldn't work that night, the powder or something was wet. They had no way of gettin' the line across. But my father – don't mind my sayin' so – was the best swimmer in the outfit.

He weighed two hundred and thirty-five, forty pounds. I'm not that small but my mother weighed a hundred and twenty. You see why I'm not big.

"But anyway, they had to tie a rope around his body. And he swam out there in that ragin' surf to the ship. And they pulled him aboard so they could get the lines. And they brought the women and children safely across on shore. They didn't lose a single passenger. Now, as a memento for that they gave my father the name plate off'n the side. A board about six seven feet long. *C.E. Newman.* And he had a storage place down in the yard and he had that tacked across there. That was one of the most eventful or historic things that happened on the coast there, at the Pea Island Station.

"That was before I was born. It was eighteen something. I guess it was ten or fifteen years before I was born.

"It was after I was born and grew up to be 'bout eleven years old, my father used to have me to come down with the man who was coming back on liberty, coming back the day before my father was due to come on liberty. I'd go down and spend the night with my father. And once I went on the south patrol with him when he was on duty there. Well, I didn't walk that patrol. They had big horses that used to haul the surfboats around. And so he took me in a buckboard. So he carried a clock with him that they would punch. Your key was down at the end of the patrol. You strike that clock, then at the keeper's station the next morning he could tell exactly when you hit that clock. Well, I went in the Coast Guard myself in World War Two and I was glad to go, for I wanted to follow in the same footsteps he had gone. And I had the same duty up in Long Island. It was a similar patrol to the one he was on when he sighted the *Newman* on shore, in a storm, on that particular night.

"I'd give anything if I had my father's picture. He was, you might say, quite a specimen of a man. One of the tests that some of the men found difficult to do he found easy. He had to dive down in six feet of water and bring up a fifty-pound weight. My father had eight gold stripes on his arm. That was for good conduct and unbroken service.

"My mother's name was White. Her father was Rowan White, her mother was Sarah White. She had about four, five sisters, and three brothers. They all grew up here. But they moved after they were grown. I had a uncle once lived in New Bern the rest of his life, and some of them went up to Hampton, Virginia; but they didn't go too far away.

"I really don't know how my people happened to come here. My father's father was John Meekins. Now a lot of the people who came here, they came from Hyde County, but most from Tyrrell County. Most of the people I knew were from Tyrrell and Washington County. I taught school in Washington County and I met quite a few people who knew people I knew when I was growing up. The short migration was from Hyde and Tyrrell. I think most of those who came to Roanoke Island came when they were freed, after the war. Maybe it was somewhat of a haven. There was a place they used to call Burnside, after General Burnside, in the Civil War. Burnside used to belong mostly to Negroes. And the fellow who owned the best land up there was Ben and Hannah Golden, which was my wife's grandfather.

"I grew up here until I was thirteen. And I was here off and on then. 'Cause I went to high school in Elizabeth City. I was there for about six years. I was here off and on and during the summer. After I finished high school I was here more infrequently, but I never stayed away more than two years at a time.

"The first thing I remember in growing up? At an early age – I suppose I must have been about seven, eight years old – when my father, I was the youngest, he took me when he was on vacation once and we went to see my oldest brother and sister, who were living in Phoebus. That was you might say the most eventful trip in that it was the first one I had leavin' the island. They had the steamboat to Elizabeth City, then we'd take the train, the Norfolk & Southern, to Norfolk. First they had a gas boat, the *Hattie Creef*, then they had the steamer *Trenton*. The *Trenton* was the main boat I took going back and forth from Elizabeth City there.

"I went to the Roanoke Academy here in Manteo until I was thirteen. It was a frame two-story building. We had hygiene, history, geography. We had the Riverside Literature and the regular Milne Arithmetic. I haven't thought of that book in years. It wasn't as standardized as it might have been. But I wasn't too far behind, when I went to Elizabeth City. They put you back a grade anyway. It has its advantages and disadvantages. You do a little bit of repeating, but some things stick better going over them a second time.

"We didn't teach the Bible as such in school. The last principal we had here was the Reverend Dickens. He was a minister, but he didn't dwell on anything too religious.

Maybe, more, morality. (Laughs.) Growing up here I went to Haven Creek Baptist Church. Our ministers were just way above par. They had been to seminaries and they were well versed in the Scriptures. I tell you frankly – well, I go to church now and I really find that some of the sermons I heard then were more educational, more revealing, and better prepared than many of the sermons I hear now.

"My mother took me to church. We had the morning service, then we had Sunday School. Then the evening service. So I went to church three times a day on Sunday. I still remember some of the texts that I learned when I was 14, 15 years old. I recall two ministers in particular. Reverend Sharp, from Edenton. And one of the best sermons I ever heard, he gave from the Eighth Psalm. I memorized it afterward:

> *Oh Lord our Lord, how excellent is thy name in all the earth! who hast set thy glory above the heavens.*
>
> *Out of the mouth of babes and sucklings hast thou ordained strength because of thine enemies, that thou mightest still the enemy and the avenger.*
>
> *When I consider thy heavens, the work of thy fingers, the moon and the stars, which thou hast ordained;*
>
> *What is man, that thou art mindful of him?*

" – And so on, I won't go on with the rest of it. That was one of the best sermons. But I gave you the wrong man. Reverend Sharp preached a sermon wonderful like that, but this was Reverend Delanie, from Washington County. But we had on our baccalaureate sermon, Reverend John Moore, and that was one of the best I ever heard. And he took his text which I remember from Jeremiah, 48th chapter, 11th verse. "Moab hath been at ease from his youth." I won't quote that. But all the worthwhile sermons – well, maybe all of them are worthwhile – but the best, they were in my earliest childhood here.

"The only game I played mostly was we played a little sandlot baseball. We usually had a homemade ball, but once in a while we had a little league baseball. But we only had one, so if you knocked it over in the bushes that stopped the game until you found it. They had a lot up here about where you see the community building out here. There weren't any houses being built up there then. We had almost two acres of playing ground. No, we never played with the white boys while I was here. They played cross town.

"When we had quite a influential speaker here we would reserve seats for part of the white congregation. One of the old gentlemen was quite a close friend of mine. Mister Acie Evans. My aunt used to cook for them. I don't know why he took a liking to me. He ran the Tranquil House downtown. That was the main hotel here then. His son Charlie was the postmaster here for a while. I knew old Charlie and his father very well. In fact Mister Evans thought so much of me he used to have me around in the floweryard as a companion for him. When grown men were gettin' a dollar a day for work, he'd pay me a dollar just for helpin' him set out flowers. Let's see, I was eleven or twelve then.

"In those days a dollar would go quite a distance. When

you only had to pay a penny for a postcard and two cent for a stamp letter a dollar would go pretty good. It was like in Depression days. When I first went to New York in '29, down in Delanccy Street on the East Side, you could go to a stand and get a kosher, strictly beef hot dog and a mug of root beer for five cent. The hot dog was full dressed with onions and sauerkraut. So you could buy a whole lot for a dollar.

"The first time I tasted liquor? Well, when my father came home from the Coast Guard station on his liberty he might have a bottle of gin. He didn't ever give me any, but I might have sneaked a little bit. Not enough to be noticed, or for it to go to my head. But he would make apple cider. We had a lot of fruit trees. See, my father had two months vacation – they would come home first of June and stay till the first of August. Unless they had a wreck or a storm, then they had to go back. But during that time my father would have us to farm. We raised everything we need. Chickens, and hogs, and all kind of crops. But he would grind up apples and make a 55-gallon drum of apple cider. Um hum. Now we could drink all that cider we wanted till he put sugar in it. Then he'd put lock and key on it. See, after you put the sugar in it ferments, and it gets as strong as your average liquor. He would save that for his company. He might let you have just a little sampling of it. But it wasn't free like it was before he made it hard. It was very delicious, but it'll slip up on you. You can become intoxicated before you realize it.

"Our farm was down there near where the Hardee's place is – that takes in part of it. It was all strictly along the highway, over a quarter mile long. Twenty-five acres, fifteen of it cleared. And you had about ten acres of woodland back of you. I would never have left that land been broken up, just in honor of my father. But you know you can't do what you want. You'll always have some members of the family are going to pull off and do things, and they wanted to sell and get rid of it. I don't know what each one got, but I didn't get anything because I was off at school. If I had stayed here and watched things we'd have it now. For whatever it sold for a different one, is worth ten times as much now.

"When I was a kid we would go down there to Mill Landing and meet my father and my uncle when they came back from the Coast Guard, and bring them home. Old man E. R. (Zeke) Daniels' store was there. He was about the wealthiest man in property on the island. They claimed Clary Pugh had more cash money, but old man Zeke had more property. He owned several boats, I think he owned the *Hattie Creef*. *Pompano* was another boat Uncle Zeke owned. I remember his son Preston well. He used to come by home flyin' on a motorcycle.

"Oh, yeah, they allowed us to go in that store. My aunt and another lady used to cook down there for him. And George Pledger, who used to live in front of us across the highway, he worked with him for just about all his life. Old man Zeke was very liberal, just like old man Acie Evans. I came home some years ago and I met his son Charlie so he said to me, he said, 'Nick, have you been over t'see my father?' I said, 'No, I haven't.' He said, 'Would you go over and see him? He's getting quite feeble. He thought so much of you, I know he'd be glad to see you.' So I went over to see him. He was just a fine old gentleman."See, some of the people were just like that. People like I'm tellin' you about, like the Evanses, the Creefs – one my very best friends was Albert Evans. His father was the blacksmith here. My father used to get him to make all his carts. He always had a nice horse cart so that during bad weather – we had to walk about a mile and a quarter from my home to the school. But when it was bad weather my brother used to drive us to school.

"My father died on October the thirtieth, nineteen seventeen. He and another man, Kitt Miller, were coming back from Pea Island in Miller's boat. And the engine quit. And the tide carried them out to sea into a storm. They said they could see them from shore for a long time. They were trying to make it back but they couldn't against the current.

"My mother was the finest little black woman I have ever known. After she was widowed she never married. She talked to a lady when my father passed, Miss Ella Dunbar, who was a teacher here, about what to do about putting me and my sister in the right place. We were the two youngest. I was twelve when my father passed, and she was fourteen. I only had one sister and five brothers. All older – I was the youngest.

"So Miss Ella Dunbar told her the best thing to do was to put my sister and me in the Normal School in Elizabeth City. 'Cause she was getting a small pension from the government because of my father's death, and till my sister and I were eighteen we would draw enough money to go to school. But my mother could not stand to see us go. She found a lovely place for us to board. Mrs Mary Hargood's. She had a big home then on Southern Avenue extension. I loved her, she treated me like her own son. My mother stayed there a few days with a friend of hers after she dropped me off. But when she got ready to leave it was all she could do to leave me. And she would come over there and get some work around the school, they had a farm there, vegetables and beans. Not that she – well, she did need the money, but she did it to be near me.

"In fact my first year at State Normal, that was at Elizabeth City, it was interrupted by the flu. We had gone there my sister and I for about two or three months and the school closed down on account of the flu epidemic. They opened up after a few months, but I didn't go back till the following year. I stayed there until twenty-five, 1925, when I finished high school.

"I enlisted in the Coast Guard the 15th of August 1942. And I stayed there exactly thirty-seven months. Here's a copy of my discharge. I was seaman first, then I changed to fireman. I wasn't anxious to go to sea, and I had a better chance to go to shore duty as a fireman. See that there? If you stayed in over three years and didn't come back late or anything you got the Good Conduct medal. Sixty-nine dollars a month. That was big money then.

"I was up in Long Island right after a German sub put those spies ashore there. I was stationed with the fellow, John Cullen, the boy who turned them in. Cullen when he intercepted those spies all he had was a nightstick. And they offered him five hundred dollars as a bribe to let 'em through. Their mission was to blow up the bridge between Newark and

New York. They said they was rumrunners. They gave him $480 – shortchanged him – and he hightailed it to the station and reported it. Within minutes they had all of Long Island cut off. I don't think they treated Cullen right. They had so many ninety-day wonders. Why in the world didn't they make him a lieutenant? What if he had just put that money in his pocket?

"When I enlisted I was working as a redcap in Penn Station. Before that I had two or three jobs. I worked as a postal clerk. That was during the Depression and I almost starved. I was a temporary sub, I only worked during the summer, and they gave me all the work. What I did was I took the examination for subway conductor and when I got out of the service they offered me either one. I could go back to the railroad or I could go there. So I went back with the railroad.

"I wore these legs out in eighteen years at the railroad. I had a family to take care of and going to school too. I went to school days from nine to three and I had to be at work at the railroad at four thirty. But every dollar counted. Every time I took a passenger to a train, or picked up a passenger, that was an extra dollar. It didn't bother me then – I could run up and down, didn't even stop to wait for the escalator.

"I'd get sometimes three passengers off the same train, they were waiting on the platform for a redcap. Sometimes you'd make two dollars a night, sometimes twenty or thirty. Some would give you a dime, some would just pay for the tags, for the railroad. The highest I had was several ten-dollar tips. But I tell you the worst job I had was Gene Tunney. He came down the station late, so another fellow, Killer Wiggins and I, we ran down to the train just as hard as we could. And just there in time to put his bags on. You know what he handed us? One dollar! Millionaire! That wasn't even enough to pay the tags. Why couldn't he have accidentally pulled out a twenty?

"I admired Jack Dempsey as much as I disadmired Tunney. When I was in service he was a lieutenant commander. He had charge of us in New York, he used to come around and inspect our work in the sail loft. Very soft-spoken, he never spoke above a low monotone. He may have been a terror in the ring, but personally he was a fine man.

"I stayed with the railroad while I went to Long Island University for three years under the GI Bill. Then I resigned and came home and did another year's work at North Carolina Central; and then I started teaching.

"I taught in Washington County for about fourteen years. The first years I taught at the local high school and the last year I was transferred to the Plymouth high school, and that's where I retired from. The Washington County school was predominantly black. After they integrated I was transferred to Plymouth. But of all the black and white students, of all the thousands I taught during those fifteen years, I didn't have more than three ornery ones. Ninety nine and nine tenths per cent were fine students I could reach. These contrary ones, they just didn't want to do their work. I remember one boy from Creswell I used to get on. He was about to fail, but I gave him a D minus to let him go. When he finished school he came and gave me his school picture. I said, 'James, I appreciate it. I guess you always felt I was being too hard on you.' He said, 'No, Mr. Meekins, I wish you'd been a little bit harder.' I was so surprised you could have knocked me down with a feather.

"I taught English and social studies. I really love literature. I took extra hours in college. For a major I needed forty some hours. I think I had seventy hours in English. I follow most of those New England writers. One of my favorites is Channing. And Longfellow and Emerson, and Theodore Parker. Hawthorne – I liked most of Hawthorne. But *The Scarlet Letter*, I liked it and hated it. Hester suffered too much.

"William Ellery Channing was one of my favorites. He was speaking about books. He said, if I can give you this:

> 'In the best books, great men talk to us, give us their most precious thoughts, and pour their souls into ours. God be thanked for books. They are the voices of the distant and the dead, and make us the heirs of the spiritual life of ages past. Books are the true levelers. They give to all, who will faithfully use them, the society, the spiritual presence, of the best and greatest of our race. No matter how poor I am, no matter that the prosperous of my own time would not enter my obscure dwelling. But if the sacred writers will enter and take up their abode under my roof; if Milton will cross my threshold and sing to me of Paradise; Shakespeare, to open to me the world of imagination, and the workings of the human heart; Franklin, to inject me with his practical wisdom; I shall not pine for want of intellectual companionship. I may become a cultivated man, though excluded from what is

termed the best society in the place where I live.'

"That's one of the best things I got from Channing.

"I tried to be emphatic, or dynamic, in my presentation of literature, and my students still ask me for 'Gunga Din' or 'The Raven' when I see them. I memorized quite a few things. Last year we went to Hatteras High School, it was Negro History Week. And they gave us such a warm welcome and asked us to come back. One of the teachers there sent me a thank you letter and forty students had signed it. I don't want to look for it now. But she said 'After you left, the students talked more about you than they did about the senior prom.' Evidently I made a pretty good impression.

"We recited some things from Negro writers. Like Kelly Miller. He was Dean of Men at Howard University. He wrote a World War One history. And one of the memorable things in it was an open letter he wrote in 1917 to President Woodrow Wilson. The other was Frederick Douglass, his speech that he made in Rochester on the Fourth of July of 1852. Did you ever read that? He said,

> *"Fellow Citizens: Pardon me, and allow me to ask, why am I called upon to speak here today? What have I or those I represent to do with your national independence?. . . To drag a man in fetters into the grand illuminated temple of liberty, and call upon him to join you in joyous anthems were inhuman mockery and sacrilegious irony."*

"He knew his Bible; he knew the lament of a woe-smitten

people, when the ancient Israelites said,"By the rivers of Babylon, there sat we down; and we wept when we remembered Zion." He thought it was rather ironic during the Fourth of July, to celebrate liberty while he had four and a half million brothers in slavery. His mistress, the white lady, taught him to read. He ran away to Baltimore and worked on the docks. But he sent back and paid for his freedom! The language that he uses is marvelous. You wonder now, how did he master such language?

"And then Paul Lawrence Dunbar, our first renowned Negro poet; he wrote a lot in dialect. Let me give you one they liked:

The Lord had a job for me, but I had so much to do.

So I said, get somebody else, or wait till I get through.

I don't know how the Lord came out, but He seemed to get along.

But I felt kind of sneaky like, 'cause I knowed I'd done him wrong.

Then one day I needed the Lord, I needed him right away.

But way down in my accusin' heart, I could hear him say,

Son, I've got too much to do; you get somebody else, or wait till I get through.

Now, when the Lord has a job for me, I never try to shirk

I drop just what I have on hand, and does the good Lord's work.

And my affairs can run along, or wait till I get through.

Nobody else can do the job that God's marked out for you.

"I was glad to take those things to Hatteras. And you know, that was the first time. I'd been far as Pea Island, and all these years I'd heard so much talk of Hatteras, but I'd never been down there.

"You know, most of my reading I did before I was eighteen years old. I read night and day. But in after years my eyes bother me. When I got in service I had 20-20 vision. But now, when I have plenty of time, I can't read more than five or ten minutes. The reading that I did before I finished high school kept me through college. So many things I had read then I could draw on. It just came in mighty handy in later years.

"My father, he wasn't a highly educated man, but he was self-educated. He bought books. One of the finest books he bought was by William Ellis, *Billy Sunday: The Man and His Message. World War History* by Kelly Miller. He had all about the Galveston Flood, Spanish-American War, the white slave trade. He read all those during his leisure time in the Coast Guard. He had some wonderful books. I wonder how he selected them. But I guess the salesman would come down to the station. I can't find them now.

"I recall he had a power boat called the *Henrietta*, after my mother. It was the best boat around there. And so we were coming across the Inlet, and he revved up the motor. And I wondered why. And about the time he revved up the motor the boat moved to the side. She had hit the current in the channel. So he caught me by the waistband and told me to look over the washboard of the ship. I looked over there and as far down as you could see the water was clear; but you could see that current cuttin' the sand from the bottom. Now little did he dream that was going to be his doom.

"Little things like that I remember about him and I'm proud. As I said, the October 30th, 1917, was my saddest day. I was at school, and there was a boy, Haywood Wise, he was my buddy since we could remember. Eleven, twelve years old. He was superintendent of the Sunday School here for thirty-five years. He passed a few years ago. Now, when the word came that my father had been blown out to sea, we had been out playin'. It hit me so I got up and went over and sat down by myself. Haywood had stopped playing and sat by me too. He didn't know what to say, but he felt my hurt was his hurt. And after that I got my books and started on that mile home. And he walked half the way with me. In Hutchinson's book *This Freedom* he says"In our successes, our hours of triumph, there are a hundred eyes that shine with ours in those. But it's defeats you want her to tell. The lights that are gone out; the springs that spring no more; the secret sordid things that hedge you in, that draw you down; those, to have somebody to tell those to." That's what a real friend means to you.

"I went on home. And my home, for the next week, which had been so quiet and peaceful, was bedlam. My mother for nights walked the floor. Maybe she was hoping against hope;

hollering and crying for nights. Aunt Victoria Daniels, Nancy Midgett, the neighbors did all they could to console her. But she didn't want to be consoled.

"I don't know why people do things like that, but a month or so later somebody put a article in the paper that Theodore Meekins and Kitt Miller had been picked up by a German tramp steamer and were making their way home. That gave us some terrible false hopes. It was a hoax. They never did find Kitt Miller, but six months later my father – what remained of my father – washed up on the beach down there between Oregon Inlet and Pea Island. And they could only identify him by his underwear and his dental work.

"I came back here September before last. After I retired I stayed in Washington County. I had so many friends there. I hadn't been in a rush to come back. I had feelings for the old homestead, but I had some unpleasant memories too. But my wife wanted to come home. She has three brothers here.

"I might say what ought to be my happiest time was when I wanted a son, and when my son was born – in fact all my children. I had two boys and three girls. I was mighty joyful about that. And thank God they've never given me any problems or trouble, and they're self-sufficient and independent. And they all went to college.

"My oldest son is in the Coast Guard. When he got out of college he enlisted in the Navy, so I got him to switch. This is his picture when he was commissioned. He flies the helicopters. This is my baby girl; she lives in Durham. My other son is in Minnesota. I have one daughter in Los Angeles and my other daughter is a nurse in New Haven. See, all of them are just as far from me as the ends of the country, but I hear from them every week.

"I have so many nieces and nephews here. Must have a hundred of them. Too many! They come to me, speak t' me, 'Uncle Nick,' and I have to get them to tell me who their mother is.

"I feel somewhat depressed when I think of how I'm unable to reach so many young people. Those kids the other day – suicides – sometimes I'm just dumbfounded. As much as I took in psychology I never really learned how to reach somebody. The human mind is so intricate! It seems the more I studied the more nonplussed I became.

"The best approach I know is to show them that, you're not alone. There's others have had greater problems than you. I had something prepared for when I went back to Hatteras. I think it would be about as good as any, come to think about it. Dwight Hillis, in *The Battle Of Principles*, has one part on Abe Lincoln. He gave it in such beautiful language. I'll try to give it to you. He said that when the country was threatened, the very existence of government, that God needed a man like Lincoln. He said,

> "*Lincoln was the man who had walked for fifty years under cloudy skies. He was the most picturesque figure in history. He was the strongest, the gentlest, the saddest, the most pathetic figure in history. God chose him. He passed by the palaces and went to a cabin in the wilderness. And he took this little baby in his arms and called to his side his favorite angel, the Angel of Sorrow. And said to him,*

'Take this little child of mine, and make him great.' Said, 'Take from him everything that he loves. As he climbs the hills of adversity, let his footprints be stained with his own blood. Till his face is more marred than any man of his time. Then bring him back to me, and I will have him free four million slaves.'

"So he said, 'God, and sorrow, made Lincoln great.' If kids could think about the problems that others have had, that they're not alone, their depression would be lifted.

"Well, my worst drug is my beer and my pipe, but I'm addicted to that TV more than anything else. Sometimes I have to crawl around on the floor to get over to it. I can't do a lot of walking, but I get stiff if I sit still too long. Hard to believe I was the captain of the football team, isn't it? I could really move then.

"I have some regrets about things I might have done differently. But you know, I don't have any real fear. Yes, I believe there's an afterlife. I tell you, there has to be. Whether it's beyond purgatory or not. If there is such a thing as Purgatory, then maybe it isn't necessary to have a Judgment, if you can be cleansed before a future life. Too much a belief in one might contradict the other. You might be punished in this world. There seems to be some judgement here. But there has to be <u>some</u> reckoning.

"I try to do like, what did William Cullen Bryant say in 'Thanatopsis' –

Thou go not, like the quarry-slave at night,

*Scourged to his dungeon, but, sustained and soothed
By an unfaltering trust, approach thy grave,
Like one that wraps the drapery of his couch
About him, and lies down to pleasant dreams."*

REMEMBER, WE DON'T GIVE UP:
Marilyn Daniels

Marilyn Daniels Midgett smokes steadily in the wheelchair. Her wide face crinkles at the eyes behind a steadily ascending ribbon, a veil; one hand steadies the filter tip, the other brushes nervously at her long hair. She's younger than some of the other patients at the nursing center in Nags Head. Younger, but she holds her head rigidly lifted, nostrils flared. The effect is both regal and stoic, a kind of imperiousness in pain. She wears a smile continuously, even when occasional tears, perhaps from the smoke, fill her eyes as she talks.

"I was born in Wanchese, May 31, 1919.

"What do I remember – well, my grandfather had this farm. And George Pledger, this old colored fella, took care of everything. He had a horse and cart. And I remember, I used to ride with him deliver groceries from the store. He'd put a plank across the cart and I'd sit up on the plank. And we had an old buggy, we went to Sunday school in the buggy.

"Growing up in Wanchese . . . each summer I would go to Elizabeth City and spend a week. We'd leave the Wanchese wharf at six o'clock on my grandfather's boat. It wasn't such a big boat, but it was big for those times. It had a cabin for the passengers, and a place where you could put a car. The wharf had planks on it where you could go up on the boat. And we had a little galley there where we'd eat supper.

"And we'd stop at – we took fish in the hull of the boat, you know, had them iced down, and we'd stop at Manns Harbor and Mashoes, and Stumpy Point, and pick up fish. We'd get to Elizabeth City at twelve o'clock that night. Yes, it took all day. Then it left Elizabeth City the next day at twelve o'clock and got to Wanchese at six that afternoon. He had two boats, the *Hattie Creef* and the *Lloyd Junior*, so they made round trips every day.

"When I was a little girl my grandfather had the boats, and he owned the Wanchese Wharf. You know where Mill Landing, that center is? Wanchese is on the other end, where Queen Anne's Revenge is. We used to have a big ice plant down there, and had the Wanchese Wharf, and there was a little office where you went in to buy your tickets to go to Elizabeth City.

"My grandfather was E. R. Daniels. They called him Uncle Zeke. Ezekiel – I don't know what the R was for. He grew up here, his people – his mother was a Skinner. My mother's name was Montague. I think really that Pop came from Currituck, but I don't know where it was before it got to Currituck. It kind of sounds like a French name.

"I reckon most of my people is English, though. They say they was washed ashore here on the boats. They'd crack up, and they would land, or be washed up on the beach. And then they'd start from there. That's why so many people I think down the Banks, so many of them are a little bit retarded. Because they intermarried. There was so much intermarrying

– cousins to cousins. What I mean is, like first cousins marrying. Course it kind of had to start that way.

"My grandfather was a nice looking man – he had a gray moustache, not a great big moustache, not one of these hangin' kind. He was very distinguished looking, I thought. But he couldn't write; he had no education; you could hardly read his name. How could he run the store when he couldn't write? Well, you've seen how people's hand are all trembly? That was like his; it was like he learned to write all by himself. Maybe he did. He could read, I think, probably. I really don't know because he died when I was twelve or thirteen.

"In the store was a little office. You'd go upstairs. That was where he sat. And they sold everything in the world in there. One side was a grocery store; and on the other side, was your underwear, and then bolts of material – you know everybody sewed then, they made their own clothes. And they had two long shelves with nothing but material, and they'd go buy two yards of this, three yards of that, to make their dresses. He had an old smokehouse there where they killed their own meat, smoked the meat, and had a little dairy house to keep the milk cool – had a little cement walk going to it.

"On the farm he had irish potatoes, and even had enough so that he could ship them out. And watermelons, and field peas, apple trees – he had just about everything. Now all that land is built up and there's twenty-five houses on it. People now are too lazy to farm.

"Everybody in Wanchese had a boat then. Down there then most of the fishing was shad fishing. Put the stakes out in the sound, and a net . . . my grandfather would lend people, feed 'em, the whole year. Each spring they would come and pay him what they owed him. And some of them, if they wanted five dollars, they'd come and draw five dollars; and then at the end of the season, if they had a good season, they would pay him. Shad was the way most of them made their living then. But they don't fish shad now. I don't know if they've all gone, or if people have quit eating them cause they got bugs in them.

"Gosh, Wanchese has sure changed. You never locked your doors down there then. You knew everybody. And then I remember, when people got sick in Wanchese, neighbors would leave their own; and if they were so sick you had to keep an eye on them, people would sit up with them all night. Take turns, you know. And they'd bring food to 'em, and take care of them. Everybody just pitched in.

"Yes, my grandfather was – I won't say he was rich, but he I know you've heard of Mr. Theodore Meekins, all the land the Meekinses had, and the Etheridges. Well, Mr. Bruce Etheridge told me that Mr. Theodore foresaw that all this was going to happen – the Beach was going to expand; and they borrowed money from my grandfather to buy a lot of this land over here. Over here on the beach, stuff that they didn't think were nothing, you know. And my grandfather was no notes or nothing, it was just his word. That you owe me this much money. I don't know how much they borrowed; not too much, I don't imagine, cause everything was cheap then. But I know Mr. Bruce Etheridge has told me many a time that my grandfather started him off, and how he didn't have to sign a note.

"My father worked in my grandfather's store. His name was Preston Daniels. Boy, I remember my daddy, he liked his booze. They'd get five gallon jugs of East Lake, they'd bring it over and hide it out in the woods somewhere. You've heard of East Lake corn whiskey, haven't you? East Lake's just a little past Manns Harbor. A lot of people are buying property there now because it's undeveloped. And it's so pretty over there . . . it'll be more valuable than this beach, because it's buildin' up too fast.

"No, I never worked in my grandfather's store. After he died – oh, gosh, after he died my uncle took over the estate and you know that when you die nobody pays their bills. All he had left was the land, I think, and my uncle got just about all of that.

"I went to school to Wanchese, to the seventh grade. After seventh grade I went to Manteo to high school. We only had eleven years of school then. I had to walk to school for the first seven years. And we walked to Sunday school – we had to go every Sunday. Methodist. If I didn't stay to church couldn't go out Sunday afternoon. In Sunday school we'd sing, and the teacher had a little quarterly she'd read, and then we'd read a verse. We sang old hymns – What a Friend We Have in Jesus, Love Lifted Me, Tell Me the Story of Jesus.

"Well, as a little girl I didn't do much else. There wasn't much to do. All I remember is going to Elizabeth City. My aunts lived in Elizabeth City. My mother would give me five dollars to spend, stay a week. I remember – to this day I still like them – I'd go to Woolworth's, and there was this big candy counter, this big thing shaped up like this of chocolate kisses. I'd buy them by the bagful.

"You know, in 1937, when we had the 350th anniversary of the Lost Colony, they made those Virginia Dare coins and they had a picture of Kill Devil Hill, the monument on one side, and on the other side the lady with Virginia Dare in her arms. A lot of people still have them. Anyway, they were trying to advertise them, so there was this radio program in New York, 'We the People' was the name of it. They got an appointment that somebody could be on this program. And so they got me to talk to the man on the telephone. They tried to say that this was the real Elizabethan language. And so I went on and talked to him and he invited me to New York. I was only sixteen, and I said I couldn't go by myself. So he said that I could have a companion, he'd pay.

"So we went! I never been so scared in my life. But we really put on the dog! I believe we stayed at the Admiralty. We sat in the hotel with our door wide open; then when we left the hotel, we'd lock her up. And we'd eat in the dining room, and before you could finish with what they'd given to you, all these fancy waiters'd take it away – and we didn't know what we were eatin'. So we found this little place round the corner where we could get a sandwich. He had us on the show, but when I got up there, I couldn't remember to talk like that. But we did get in on it that we came from Dare County.

"I got married in forty-six. I was old enough to know better. I worked at Hubby Davis's. That was a country store at Wanchese that sold everything, and that also had the post office in it. The post office was a little corner, it had boxes across, at this time you had to call for your mail. And I worked there till I went to work for the post office in Manteo.

"Mr. Davis left me a ten-dollar gold piece when he died. I saw it one time and he promised it to me. He gave it to his brother for me, and he gave it to one of the clerks. And the night he died, the next day she brought it to me. 'Here,' she said, 'I want to get rid of this.'

"During the war I worked at the post office. I went to work there in forty-four. The year of the storm – we had a real bad one that year.

"I was a clerk. Our postmaster got cancer and was real sick. And when he was sick I took his job. I didn't get recognition but I did his work. Back then at the post office instead of going and opening their box everybody'd ask you to get it for them. You had to wait on them. It wasn't nothing like it is now. When I was there we had six hundred and seventy-five postal boxes to rent. And somebody told me the other day they have sixteen hundred now and they don't have enough.

"And you know, I can't remember when I retired? Seems like it was in '71 or '72. I had almost thirty years then. They passed a rule that you could retire if your years of service and your age amounted to eighty. With a reduced annuity.

"I met my husband in Manteo, at a little drug store. His name was Robert. His father was in the Coast Guard. Well, we got along real fine, he was real good to me. And then in seventy-five I fell and broke my hip. Went to the hospital. And there was a little girl from India there, a nurse, she'd been over about three weeks. And she and my husband kind of fell in love.

"I think it just started out, she was real lonesome, and she'd come in my room and cry, and read letters from her father to me; and then I'd tell him how pitiful she was, and this and that, and one afternoon he took her home. Which I didn't think anything about it, because she was twenty-six and he was sixty-two. But anyway it kind of went on, and maybe she didn't think anything about him, but he did. And I got so sick they sent me to Chapel Hill. I was there for three months. And for that time they were together more and more.

"So I came home, and I lived there a year. I felt like a vase sitting on a wall – I felt like something that had to be fed, had to be watered. He was good to me, doing everything, and he waited on me, but I knew that I was in the way. And on her days off, he would leave, go off and spend the day with her. And he'd leave early in the morning before I got up. It was kind of bad on me. But I finally made up my mind that when I got up on that walker a little bit, so I could get up and go to the bathroom by myself, that I would get me an apartment.

"And so I told him, I remember I waited till the World Series game was over, and then I told him that I had rented an apartment and that I was leaving the next morning; that I had some people to help me move. Only thing that worried him was my brother. He wanted my brother to know that he hadn't asked me to leave. He had a lot of respect for my brother – I think more than he had for me. So he went and had a talk with him about it. Everybody knew what was happening, but they wouldn't talk to me about it, and I wouldn't talk to them. I just didn't want to talk about it.

"Then people would come in and he'd tell them how he couldn't leave Marilyn, he hated to leave Marilyn, and then the next day he'd go off and leave me to myself. He really changed. He wasn't living with her, I reckon; I don't know what they were doing. I don't think he was courtin' her much, 'cause by then he was sixty-five.

"Anyway, I left on the sixth of October, and he stayed there till May, I think. Then he moved to Butler, North Carolina. She got a job there. It's a federal thing where they treat alcoholics and teach braille, and retarded children. So he moved up there, and has a job in some mill factory. As a caretaker or something. He claims – he's told me so many stories I don't know if I can believe him – he's told me she was married. That her husband came back with her from India and he was four foot tall and weighed a hundred and ten pounds. That was all he said about him.

"Something just happened to him – second childhood, or love, or something. And right at the end he just imagined things. He heard voices, he could hear people talking out in the yard, they were going to kill him, somebody was going to get him. I still haven't told him what I believe t'was; he'd been so sneaky, trying to do all this stuff to prevent me from knowing it, then he felt everybody else was doin' him the same way. I think you can get like that – you can be so sneaky yourself that you don't trust anybody.

"'Course I hear from him now and then. I get a Christmas present every Christmas. Don't have a divorce, say he don't want a divorce. I've thought about getting that, but then I've thought in my condition to go to court, probably have a fuss and a fight – because he built the house, before we were married, still I think I probably have a lifetime right there, I don't think he could do anything about it. As long as we're married I don't think he could sell it or anything. The first year he was gone I got a little boy and kept it mowed, but it's not rented out, he's just letting it go. It's a shame for the neighbors to have a place like that.

"Then I had to give up my apartment. I started having rectal abscesses real bad. I kept the apartment three months, thinking I was going to get back to it, and then my brothers packed up all my stuff.

"No, I had no children, thank the Lord. (Chuckles). As it is, I don't have anything to worry about, and there's nobody to worry about me. You see so many people here that their children don't come see them, and it hurts them, and so I'm glad I didn't have any. I have a niece, nephews, two brothers. And I have a lot of friends. My oldest brother was a professional prize fighter. Maynard Daniels. He was one of the first marines that landed on Guadalcanal. Now he's retired as a chief engineer from the Geodetic Survey. He lives in South Nags Head. My other brother is retired on disability; he was in the Coast Guard and the Merchant Marines. Yes, we're seagoing people around here. My nephew just joined the Coast Guard. He was working in Wilmington, the manager of a bar there, making good money. Lord knows, he quit and joined the Coast Guard! Got his wife pregnant, and he's not making the money he made. But he's planning on getting more schooling, so maybe it'll turn out good for him.

"I'm really thankful for my life. But I haven't had any real bad times. Not *real* bad. The worst thing was when my health went. But I'm thankful there, it could be so much worse. Well, my husband and all that, you know . . . but I was kind of proud to be big enough to overcome it. Course it hurt. When I moved out, my doctor said I was depressed. And I said, I'm not depressed now, when I was depressed was when I was livin' at home with him. I said, Since I've left, and in this apartment, I was just – released – the pressure was gone. Because I knew then that everything anybody done for me was because they wanted to do it. And I didn't mind askin' people. But when I was living at home with him, I didn't ask anybody, because he was supposed to be the one I should ask. But I'm real thankful for being what I am.

"My best time was high school. You didn't have as many worries, you was out jitterbuggin' and dancing. All night. And there at the end you were getting half tight every night. Going out and having fun. And then my courting days were a lot of fun. We'd go somewhere Saturday night to a party, or at that time they were having big bands over to the Casino, which was a big dance place in Nags Head. And I consider them were the happiest days, when I was in high school.

"I played basketball in high school. We'd play outdoors; the court was marked off with chalk. And you could have three forwards on this end and three guards, and three guards and three forwards on the other end. And we couldn't cross the center line. You could run all over the court, but you couldn't cross the center. And the girls couldn't dribble but one time. And I was a guard, and all I could do was keep the girl from shootin'. I couldn't try to make a goal.

"We'd play Camden and Old Trap, places around Elizabeth City. People in the community would take us in their cars. Three or four to a car. We'd leave Friday afternoon and spend the night at those places, at some of the girls' homes. We'd play Friday evening at one school, then on Saturday morning we'd play another school. You'd have to play in cold weather, goose bumps on you. And we didn't have warmup suits then either! We wore little black shorts, they were suede like. I don't know how many years they'd been used. And a white shirt. Then when we had the tournament, that would be held in Elizabeth City, indoors, and we weren't used to playing on that floor. We'd get skinned. And we weren't very good. I remember when I was in the hospital this girl wrote me a letter. She said, 'Remember, Marilyn, we don't give up. Remember the time Central beat us 57-0. But we kept on going.' So she said, 'I know you're going to keep on going.'

"But we did have fun.

"See, that was in thirty-two, cause I graduated in thirty-six. 'Cause we just had our class reunion last spring, and I couldn't go. Three of them came over to see me, though.

"Yes, I was popular in high school. I've always been blessed with good friends and getting along with people.

"I started smoking in high school. You couldn't smoke in school grounds, you know. So we smoked on the school bus, and snuck around. I remember one time I had a cigarette in my shirt pocket and I bent down and it fell on Miss Sawyer's toes. Lorraine Sawyer, she was the basketball coach.

"I dated some of the sailors during the war, but not too much. I was courted by the same one about all that time. By Robert. What did you do when you courted? You hugged, and kissed. Smooched, they call it now! And you'd always be two or three couples to a car. Everybody didn't have cars then, you know. You'd all be together, so you didn't have much chance to get off by yourself.

"That's one thing that happens to all them little kids today, I think – all having cars. They get out of school and they all take their girlfriends and go off for the afternoon. And it's just not good for 'em to be by theirselves. That's why we got so many young mamas, I think. It's real natural, and the mothers don't seem to understand. I reckon they trust them. They think, that's not going to happen to my child. But now, you know, people don't think anything about it. It's still wrong, but in the eyes of the people now it doesn't seem wrong.

"Yes, I've seen a lot of changes. We used to go to the – my uncle used to take us to the movies, to Manteo. And it cost twenty cent to get in and you had a nickel to spend. So that was a quarter. That was the late twenty-nines or thirties, I reckon. Every Saturday night, Uncle Ross would fill up the car with all little children, and take them to the movies.

"You get to thinking about things like that, you don't think that was much, but then when you get here you get to thinking about what good fun you really did have. I used to think my folks were kind of strict on me. What bothered me more than anything else was, I used to want to wear my Easter dress Saturday night to the movies. But it was new, and you weren't supposed to wear it anywhere else but to Sunday school. And then you'd come home you had to take it off and hang it up till next Sunday, till you got another new dress. I cried and I cried. And I said, If I ever got old enough to make my own money, if I wanted to scrub the floor in my Sunday dress I was goin' to do it! And I did – I wore my best dress to work, and I wore it to church too. I'd wear whatever I wanted to, because I always remembered how aggravated I'd get.

"That's right many years ago, you know. I'll be sixty-eight the last day of May. But there's time's I don't feel like I'm that old. To me, when I was a child, somebody sixty was real old; they just didn't think like young people. And now I still understand young people. Why they like to get out and do things. I'd be out there with them, yes, I would.

"Around here we play bingo on Mondays and Thursday nights. And we have a little choir at ten o'clock on Tuesdays. And we have arts and crafts in the morning. And every Sunday morning the Baptist church from Manteo has Sunday school over here. I'm Methodist, but I go to Sunday school here cause ain't no Methodists here.

"We got a new minister, and as long as this place has been here, he's the first one that's started Sunday school. The old people, they enjoy it; a couple comes over and sings with their guitar; and it's surprising, they'll be quiet and listen. Now some of them are kind of bad, but most of the time they're quiet when they talk to them. They love to sing. What do we sing? We sing the same old things. And then every Tuesday at three o'clock we have Bible study. Fella from Manns Harbor comes over. He's a retired colonel, Air Force, and he had a heart attack after he retired and he found the Lord . . . one day this little old lady, she said, 'I want to ask you, Preacher. Do you really believe there's a Hell?' And of course he said he did.

"It's kind of hard to understand, isn't it? And they sing that song, God Is So Good. But I can't see that I have to suffer as much as somebody who's been out here and killed fifteen people. Sometimes those people are crazy, they don't know what's going on, but some people have just done mean things, like stealing, deliberately. Don't seem like we'd all have to suffer the same, when we haven't done the same.

"Well, I reckon I'm wearing you out. You say you're going down to Avon? They'll be able to tell you all about the old days there."

I'LL DO WHAT I CAN:
Roland F. Stowe

The day is blustery, late October; the sky over Hatteras is gray as a gull's back, and the sea is trying once again to break through the dunes. The wind is freighted with sand, and the sea-birds have a hard time making their way against it.

The Sea Breeze Weave Shop is a white-shingled cottage just before the ferry landing in Hatteras Village. Just inside the peeling screen door the shelves of a small plank-floored showroom are crammed with carved wooden toys, woven basketry, and hundreds of rag rugs. To the left an old dog lies curled up, flicking up her eyes sleepily as you pass. Take three steps in, to the right – three steps, a left turn, two steps, and then feel your way through the door.

Roland Stowe sits on a bench in the storeroom, keeping the LaClerc loom in steady motion. He's five feet eight, getting a little heavy, wearing white shirt and red suspenders and gray Nike running shoes. His hair is pure white, like bleached cotton. Down with the treadle, pass the shuttle through, up with the treadle. The loom, one of three in the room, clanks steadily as he talks. He's been a weaver for thirty-three years. He started three years after he went blind.

"The way things were back when I was a boy here . . .

right here where I live now, this house, you couldn't sit on the porch here and see the Sound. There was only one place in the yard where you could see the water. The yard was covered with cedar trees; red cedar. And over where these houses is on the sound side there was trees growing over there, all along that side. And there was a house a little farther up, over next to the sound; it was surrounded with oak trees and fig trees and all such as that. Most of the big trees was oaks and cedars, and the figs was orchard figs. And the house across from the shop there, on the other side of the road, there was so many trees around it that the only thing you could see walking down the road was the chimney.

"Then the hurricane in '33 got part of them, then the one in '36 got the rest.

"First of my people come to Ocracoke Island in 1678. Stowes. That was on my father's side. There was a man, Joshua A. Stowe, bought two hundred acres of land on Ocracoke Island, and another two hundred at Rodanthe, or Chicamacomico as it was called back then. For forty pounds, from the Queen of England. He came from Stowe's Castle, on Richard Grenville's estate in England. And that was in 1678. All the Stowes I've ever had any contact with came from here on the Outer Banks. Their ancestors moved from here; some of 'em went inland, some went up North. The Stowes that owned all them mills in Connecticut and Rhode Island; then Herbert Stowe, or his father, moved the mills down to Belmont. Harriet Beecher Stowe was one of that family.

"And on my mother's father's side, the Odins. Now they spelled it ODIN up till back in the late twenties, thirties, some of them changed it and started spelling it ODEN. My people still spell it ODIN. And the first one of them, John Odin, he was shipwrecked here three different times. And the last time he stayed and married a Stowe. Lovie was her name. That was in 1820 when he settled here.

"Yes, he was a sailor, and of course after he stayed here he had ships. He run, he did, and then his son afterwards, here to Baltimore, and then on up to Bath, Maine. Back in them days they went on what they called the Molasses Run. The ships would go south, down to St. Kitt, and come back loaded with molasses. Most of them, they run north to Baltimore and around, they run brick and lumber out of Carolina that way.

"But back when I was a boy, everything came to Hatteras by boat. And they didn't have no harbor here; the boats and things, they anchored them all out along the shore. Right straight off here. They had what they called the fish houses, where they bought fish and landed stuff, was built out into the Sound. Just a straight building with an A roof on to it, but there was some almost sixty, seventy feet long, twenty-four, thirty feet wide, and along like that. But the boats and those was kept out along the shore here, had stakes where they put out and tied their boats to them.

"They run the Sound, mostly from here to Washington, Elizabeth City, New Bern; sometimes to Norfolk, and runs like that. You could go along the shore here, and the first boat you would see was a schooner boat name of *Virginia Dare*. That model there on the wall is of a schooner boat. And on further up was the *Milton S. Lankford*, that was a big bugeye; and then there was the *Alma White, Thomas Taylor;* the *Alma*

White was a schooner boat, *Thomas Taylor* was a bugeye. Then farther on up there was another schooner boat by the name of *Kathleen*.

"Then farther on up there was another big boat, a big bugeye, name of *Frank Falsom*. You know what a bugeye is? They were made out of two logs, y'know, bolted together. Then all the small fishing boats and things like that were here.

"I didn't work on the boats till after I finished high school. They had done away with all the sailboats then; all the schooners and bugeyes. And then they had power boats that they run from here.

"I was born July 17, 1916. I was born in the house up where my brother lives, the old homestead; we use it mostly for a storehouse now. We live right across the road from it. But when I was small, in World War One my daddy was in the Navy, and we stayed down here with my grandparents till he came back.

"I had one sister and four brothers; there was five of we boys. Roland, Dexter, Melvin, Levin, then Caleb. My sister Irene had polio when she was two years old and died from it. Caleb, his son is the eighth Caleb Ballance Stowe that's been on the island. He goes by Caleb Ballance Stowe, Junior. Only the oldest and youngest of we boys was ever married. There's three of us living now.

"Well, the first thing I remember, I was about two, two and a half year old, and my uncle and I were playin' out in the yard. And he had a hammer or maul or something and I was holding something for him to hit; and he missed it and hit my finger . . . the next thing I can actually say I remember was one time my grandfather was keeping me and my cousin. And there was a preacher holding a revival here and I remember, well, I done some little thing and my grandfather spanked me. And I remember I looked up at the preacher and said,"Mister Preacher, Pop spanked Roll."

(Chuckles.) "My brothers and them, they still call me Roll. I go by the name of Roll, and Frank, and Jimmy, and all kind of different names. Back during the war I even went by the name of Tojo. We all had names for each other. They called me Tojo, and then there was another fella I used to run around with they used to call him Downwind Jackson – he used to be in the comics, years ago.

"Did we have any fun? Why, yes, we had the time of our lives growing up. Let's see, back when I was eleven, twelve years old there was eleven small stores here on Hatteras. At one time there was two poolrooms, three dance halls, and two theatres. There was three dance halls, right there where the Atlantic View Motel is, three of them there in a cluster.

"They used to like to dance over in Ocracoke. And like in Ocracoke, they used to make meal wine. They'd take four pounds of meal and four pounds of sugar, and one yeast cake and four gallons of water, and let it work off. Then you strain it, and maybe if you want to put grapes or something like that in to it, and add a little more sugar, and let it work off again . . . Back when they used to make so much corn whiskey, it was all around East Lake, over in there. That's where all them businessmen around Manteo got their start, makin' bootleg whiskey. Vernon Davis was tellin' Levin and I one day that he'd run it as far as Chicago by the truckload. And they got five dollars a gallon for it. There was never no problem to get whiskey on Hatteras back in them days. You could buy it from bootleggers here, all you wanted for fifty cent a pint. They'd go to East Lake and get boatloads and bring it back. Levin, when he was a kid he made his money out of sellin' pint bottles to them. Saved every pint bottle they found, washed it out and sold it to the bootleggers. Five cents a bottle. Then Saturday night come you could go to the movie.

"And then baseball, there was a lot of that here. Every town had a team.

"I went to high school here. The school used to be here; then they consolidated and built the school at Buxton. I graduated in 1933.

"After that I went to work for my daddy. He owned a big freight boat, passenger boat, run from here to Washington, N.C. Well, a big boat then, she was seventy feet long. Had a big diesel motor in it. The name of her was *Mary Fletcher*. That was the name she was registered by when m'daddy bought her. And I went to work for him, twenty dollars a month.

"No, I never was mate or nothing. I just went on there and – well, I mostly cooked. You cooked beans, and meat, and fish, and vegetables. Had hot biscuits for every meal, three times a day. Just cooked ordinary like you would at home. Only didn't have lunch, but you had a full dinner if the weather was so you could cook. The galley was up in to the bow of her and 'twas right big. Had a wood cook stove and table and all that in there. And there was two bunks. One person always slept up there. I never did, I always slept in the bedroom. The cabin right back of the pilot house, it was a bedroom, and it had two bunks in it. I went for a while with my father, and then I went to work with my grandfather. He bought fish for S.P. Willis and Brothers in Washington, and then we bought for Potter Fish Company in Belhaven.

"Daddy's boat burned in thirty-five. Then he went on the boat that run from here to Engelhart for about a year. And then he went captain of the *C.H. Mallison*, from here to Elizabeth City.

"Then I started fishing and shrimping. During the war I was fishing. A fisherman. When they were sinking the ships off here, this and the other. Oh, yes, I saw that; you could sit right in the yard and see that. See the ships torpedoed, and the smoke in the air, and the explosions. That morning them two ships run together off Cape Henry, it knocked me off my feet. I was walkin' up the road. A ammunition ship and a ship full of airplane fuel run together. They found one man's hand fifty miles away, they claim, landed on the deck of a ship.

"I started having trouble with my eyes when I was eleven year old. I went on, finished high school; and I worked, fishing, shrimping, things like that until 1950. I was thirty-four year old. And then I quit, it was getting kind of dangerous working on a boat, no better than I could see. And I went to the rehabilitation center, for the blind, at Butner, North Carolina.

"Well, when I first started having trouble, they said it was the optic nerve. They didn't know too much back in them days about stuff like it. And then later they said I had retinitis pigmentosa, detached retina. And I went out there to the rehabilitation center, and then I worked for the state for about two years. I went around to different mattress shops that were operated for the blind for the Lions Clubs. I worked first in Durham, then in Asheville, and then Charlotte, and then the last place was Winston-Salem. At Durham we made mattresses mostly for Sears, and in Asheville they was making mattresses for the Air Force, the Army and things, mostly. And then of course they sold mattresses locally too.

"Well, I was like everybody else; at first I was down and out about it. But my doctor there told me, Son, it's something you're going to have to live with. You might never go completely blind, and you might wake up tomorrow morning and be totally blind. See, they didn't have all the instruments and stuff they have these days.

"So I made up my mind, well, if that's the way it's going to be, that's the way it's going to be, and I'll do what I can.

"Oh, I don't know how long it took me to come to that; wasn't long. And I got along, went around, and I went with the other people; we'd go to the dance halls, beer joints, places like that. I was all right as long as I was inside; and I went out, somebody would walk up and take a hold of my arm, go to the car, and part of the time I didn't know who it was. They never said nothing, hardly ever; once in a while somebody would make some remark, but most people don't.

"And I decided, well, I'm going to do what I can. So I wrote to Hadley School and took the correspondence course and learned to read Braille. Well, I would sit in the room at night with no lights on and read that Braille. And people might think it was funny, but me sittin' in the dark readin' with my fingers it still hurt my eyes. Now that's foolish, but it's true. I've had a lot of people say the same thing, when you're first – you know.

"Now, I could read Braille when I went to the rehabilitation center. Because there was nobody around here had ever – well, most of them had never seen any Braille. And when I got them books they'd say, oh well, you'll never learn that. I had pneumonia that January, this was back in the forties, and while I was recovering I got this course, to learn to read it. It had the letters, you know, raised, and I'd read it off to my brother, he'd write it down, I'd mail my lessons in. Yeah, those big loose-leaf binders there in the corner, they're the Bible. Braille's in three different grades, one, two, and three, and now they have a grade four, but use that mostly same as shorthand. And they figured that each grade was supposed to last six months. And I started them in January and finished them all and got my certificate in August.

"And so then the next thing, I took correspondence Bible course, from the Moody Bible Society.

"I know a lot of people that is gone and done and made good, and being blind is like anything else. It's troublesome, it's a problem, but it is not a handicap. You might not be able to see, but you can go and do and make good the same as anybody else can. There's always an opportunity for everybody.

"Back then, making mattresses, all they paid was seventy-five cent an hour. In 1951 and 1952. I told my wife – I was married in fifty-one, I met her at the rehabilitation center. Her name was Hazel. She died in 1980. She was a small woman, about four feet nine inches. And I told her, if we're going to work for nothing – well, that's what we were getting; after we paid for room and board each week we had four dollars left. That was to buy you clothes, and to buy your extry with – I smoked a pipe then.

"So after that I quit working and came back home. And I started making belts, and pocketbooks, and stuff like that. Going around from house to house, selling them. And then I got a loom and started weaving rugs. I started in May of fifty-four and I'm still at it.

"What got me into weaving? Well, when I was at the rehabilitation center I made one rug on the loom and I liked it. And so I decided I'd try it. The state furnished me a loom and materials to start with. A lady came down and helped me and my wife set them up the first time. And then after that we done it ourselves. And for the last fifteen years or so my brother's helped me. Levin's retired – he had a heart attack in '73.

"And so I learned to weave. Then in '56 the Lions Club gave me eight hundred dollars towards building the shop. And I started selling stuff, candy and drinks and ice cream, cigarettes, all such as that. But the rug business got to where it took more room; and people would come in and buy a drink and spill it on something, and I'd lose more than I would gain. So I threw my ice cream machine out the door and gave my drink box to the VFW, quit fooling with all that stuff.

"Then in 1956 I went into Edenton, to the Methodist conference that was held there, and I was ordained as a lay speaker. Could speak at any Methodist church anywhere in the world. And I bought my books that I was supposed to have, and my brother read to me at night. And then I went to Elizabeth City and took the examination, and in 1957 I was licenced as a Methodist preacher by the bishop there.

"I've been preaching part time ever since. The last few years I haven't been doing so much of it because I had two heart attacks, but I've been teaching Sunday School, men's Bible class, thirty-one years this past June. It's known as Roland Stowe Bible Class. I taught for a while and then I told them one time, well fellas, I think I've been teaching this class too long. I think you should get someone else to teach, so I'm going to quit. There was about twenty in the class; and nobody spoke. So then I started on out. Outside the door the men was all gathered out there and Ross Burris, who had Burris's Motel up here, come and took me by the arm and said, 'Come here, I want you.' I walked on over to where they were all standing, and he said, 'Well, we have talked it all over and made our decision.' I said, 'What's that?' And he said, 'Well, we have drafted you as Sunday School teacher, and we don't want to hear no more of that quittin' stuff.' So I'm still teaching.

"And I still preach when I'm called on to. Most of the time I preach from the Gospel according to John. And the Book of Romans, they're my favorite in the New Testament. And I like to teach the Old Testament. A lot of people don't, but I always did. Fact, I've always been a lover of history. History and literature was two subjects I always liked.

"I spend my nights mostly either listening to books on tape or else reading Braille. I get the different religious magazines – I get *Christian Record*, the *Lutheran Messenger*, and I get the *John Milton Magazine*. I like sea stories. I read a murder story last week. And last night I had a spy story – *A Season of Treason*. I wish they'd put more books in Braille than they got. I read most anything comes along. Except these outer space stories and all such as that. I like Shakespeare and Browning. I always liked Kipling's writings. I learned about women from Kipling's poem "Her." I never cared for Scott. Back when I was in high school I had to study *The Lady in the Lake* and I never did much care for it.

"These boxes are my stuff for the shop. Baskets and toys and stuff that I sell out there. Everything I sell in the shop is made by blind people.

"See, the State used to have the wholesale business, and I bought from them. Then last year the new governor claimed that to save money on the deal, he put them out of business. They put the men that worked there on other jobs, and still got the building rented, still keep it . . . the only thing they got rid of was two trucks that went around and picked up stuff that people had made. They sold everything, marked up a fifteen per cent profit on to it, and I don't see where they were losin' any money. And so the fellow let me know they were closing it out, and I bought six thousand dollars worth of stuff. I already had a shop full of stuff, so I had to stack it in here, in the back room.

"Business has not been so good this year as it was the last, but it's good. I can't complain. The main thing is, it gives me something to do. I'm drawing Social Security now. I don't get much, two hundred and forty-nine dollars a month, and it don't go far. So I have to work. And I enjoy it. I know people, and I get cards from everywhere. I started this in '54; I didn't have a shop, I sold things off the porch here. And the first year I had sold rugs to people in forty-two states, Canada, England, France, Switzerland, and Siam. And that was thirty-three years ago! Not this past summer, but the summer before, one morning there were people from five different countries, not counting the United States, there in the shop at one time. They were all talkin' and laughin', and said, 'We got a regular little UN here.'

"And I've been running this shop thirty-three years, and I've been taking personal checks from people all over the United States and Canada. And I've never got a bad check. I don't know how many thousands that is, but during the summertime it's nothing to have four or five hundred dollars of checks a week. One time I got one check, in the sixties, when I sold ice cream. The ice-cream man stopped in and I gave him the check. The next week I went to the mail in the morning, I had a letter from that lady. She told me when she'd got home she'd overdrawn, and to run the check through again if it came back. He come on in, he said, 'Mr. Stowe, this check come back.' I said okay, pushed the letter over to him; he read it, put the check back in his billfold, and that was the last of that.

"I have in that length of time come up short of money when I counted up in the evening twice. One time, I'm pretty sure what happened. Man laid the money on the counter, and we were talking, and I put his change up there, and it laid there, and I think by him not noticing it he picked the twenty-dollar bill up along with his change. Unintentionally. From then on, whenever anybody lays a bill down I put it in the drawer before I make change. The other time, I don't know whether I made a mistake in making change, or the boy that was working with me made a mistake. I'm sure of one thing, he didn't take a penny.

"No, no way I can tell between a twenty and a one. Lot of people claim they've known people that can. But there's no way you can because it's all made out of the same material. They tried to get them to mark the bills, put a Braille mark on them, but . . . there was a man out in Gastonia, he was born blind, been blind all of his life; he run a store there; and he could tell. I don't know how, but everybody said you couldn't fool him. But I can't, and there's a lady who run a restaurant and all, over here in Syler City, and she said she'd a lot of times she would come up forty or fifty or sixty dollars short, when people would give her bills and tell her it was something else.

"I've always felt that most people are honest. And then on the other hand, there's a lot of people just as honest as can be and straight in every way, except where money's concerned.

"Yes, I've known people that was just as nice, truthful, dependable, every way you want to come along except that if they were going to get by beatin' you out of a dollar they were going to do it. Well, I don't know why. There's a lot of difference between makin' money and takin' money. 'Cause when you short-change somebody, or get something from somebody and don't pay it, that's the same as taking it out of their pockets. But if a person pays what you charge for something, well, that's different. If I got something out there that cost me a dollar and I sell it for five dollars, if that man pays me five dollars I'm not taking him for nothing. That's the market value of it.

"But most people are honest. And yes, I consider myself honest. If I've ever deliberately beat a person out of a dime I don't know it. Now sometimes I have shortchanged people, not intentionally, but not paying attention to what I done. And a lot of times I'll give people too much. Be talking while I'm making change.

"Oh, yeah, little things I can remember. I can remember how the place was and everything here better than – I'll say sixty-five years; when I was five years old. I can remember how the island was, all such as that. In fact the road wasn't paved. It was paved from here to Rodanthe in the forties, it was never put across the game reservation up there till fifty-two. That was the biggest change.

"And the change has been for the worse, not for the better. Too much building. Too many people. Fact, even five years ago, six, if you left something out on the porch, or out in the yard, it would stay there until you went and got it. Now if you don't lock your doors and lock everything up it won't be there. Last week my brother had a bicycle in the carport up there, he brought me down here and went on to Manteo, and he was back home at eleven, and somebody stole his new bicycle in that length of time.

"And they go around in vans and things, and they poke around and look and see what they can see, and if you don't lock it, it will be stole. In the daytime or night. Shoot! Up until '52 I didn't have a lock on the front door of this house. I started leaving, going out to Gastonia in November and stayin' till March, that was where my wife was from, we'd close up Thanksgiving and go out there and stay till long 'bout the first of March every winter, and I put a lock on the door. But I'd go off, and you could stay for months at a time and leave stuff out here on the porch, around the yard, nobody'd ever touch it.

"My plans for the next few years are more of the same old thing. Levin and I, we like to go out and visit down South Carolina, down in the Fort Mills area. Next month we'll go to Wilmington for a week. Then we'll go to Smithfield for Shriners ceremonial. And I belong to the Blue Lodge, Masonic lodge here in Hatteras, Cape Hatteras Lodge, 698; the York Rite in Elizabeth City, the Shriners in New Bern, and the Scottish Rite in Wilmington.

"I plan to stay at the store as long as I can, but I have arthritis real bad. Sciatica. I certainly hate to have the cold weather come. I've had two heart attacks; in December of '85 I had congestive heart failure, I was in the hospital for ten days; and then this year I went back in the hospital and stayed eleven days with congestive heart failure again. So I'll be active just as long as I can, anyway.

"No, I don't work too hard; but see, when you're weaving you're working both arms and both legs, both feet, all the time. But I've cut down on the weaving. Most of the time I come down and open up six or seven. And I'll work until eleven, on the loom and waiting on customers, and then I'll come to the house and lie down for at least half an hour, sometimes an hour. Then I go back and I may make one rug, but I don't do much in the afternoon.

"To weave a rug, it only takes about an hour. But gettin' your material ready takes more time than it takes to weave it. Then you have to break them off and tie the fringes at the end, and all such as that. I tell people it takes me about three hours.

"I think everybody is put here for a purpose. You don't always fulfill the purpose, but there you are. When I started out I was all thrilled, I was going to preach, be an itinerant preacher. I got my license and all, and I been preaching some, but it's been right here on Hatteras Island, mostly. And I never tried to get a church, or anything like it.

"But I finally come to the conclusion that my purpose was to do just what I've been doing for the last thirty years. Work in the church right here, teach Sunday School class; I've been president of the Methodist men this is the third time around. And I don't know but what I've done more good right here on Hatteras than if I'd been pastor of a church, moving from place to place. I've had a lot of people who've told me, 'You've had more influence on my life than anybody in my whole life.' And so I think everybody's put here for a purpose.

"I don't believe a person's ever satisfied if they're doin' something they don't want to do. Now I'm doing what I want to do. But so many people today are working on jobs for the dollar, to make the money, and they're just as dissatisfied as can be. They're not interested in their jobs, they're not doing as good a work, because they want to do something else. They know what they want to do, but they're not doing it.

"A lot of people know from the time they're a child what it is they intend to do. And a lot of people don't. And I think that not knowing what they want to do, and being dissatisfied a lot of the time, leads to people drinking alcohol. And most of the time they're just as smart and well-educated people as you could find.

"I've had a lot out of preaching, and I got a lot out of the Masonic Lodge. Just stop and think about what the Masons is doing – hospitals, orphanages, old people's homes, the blind research in Boston. You read a lot of books against Masonry, but the only thing you can attribute that to is people's ignorance. If you're not in the Masons you don't know what it's all about. I've been a Mason for eight years. And my brothers, my grandfathers, my uncles. Masonry is not a religion, but it's religious. It's based on the Bible. The first question you're asked when you join is 'In whom do you put your trust?' And if the answer's not 'God' that's as far as you get. You have to believe in God and you have to believe in life after death. And the two things that the Masons teaches is the fatherhood of God and the brotherhood of man.

"Well, you want to see the looms. This is it, put that chair down there. They're the hand looms. I have three. Made by LeClerc, made in Canada. They're what you call balance looms. All wooden, all hand-operated. I don't think one ever wears out. Because if anything goes wrong, you take a piece of string that breaks and tie it up and go on. That's the shuttle, you pass it back and forth. This is the reed, this is the harness, this is the warp, and that is the woof; and that's the headle. These pedals down here, they're called treadles. It takes about two hours and a half to put the warp on. About three, that loom over there. And then I put the rugs on here . . . and you roll all that thread on and you put it through here and through here." (Begins to work loom)."You tie it down here. And right here where that pin is – see that pin? That's the beginnin' of a rug. And right there, that open space, you cut them apart.

"I usually put twelve or fourteen rugs on this one, and that one over there you put nine or ten larger ones. And the placemat one over there you can put thirty. Yes, I can tell the difference between the colors; like I told a lady in here once, I was showing her the different colors, and she said, 'how can you tell,' and I said, 'I may be blind, but I ain't stupid.' I can tell by feel . . . .

"This girl here is Pat, she's looping. Those are heels and toes they cut off from the socks. They come from the mills. I buy from Kings Mountain and Denton, and this last lot came from Bat Cave, Asheville. You knot them loops together and that's how the rugs start out. Uh-oh, I've just run out. Where is that thread?

"Have you ever drunk any East Lake corn? Good corn whiskey's hard to beat. Let me get by you into the cupboard there . . . can you get the top off of that jar. That's some of C.A.'s white lightning.

"But things is sure changed...."

LOOKING OUT FOR M'SELF:
Inez Gaimel Beacham

"Oh, I don't remember anything. I'm too old, I forgot everything I ever did know. But if you – well, it won't do you much good, but you can come over if you want."

The nonstop hysteria of construction and tourism, fast food, malls, and motels that is Route 158 Bypass drops behind with startling suddenness a few hundred yards down Old Kitty Hawk Road. The road meanders along leisurely, dipping gradually toward the Albemarle. We pass a modest post office, a Methodist church. Then there are only houses, most of them white, white clapboard, with big screened-in porches against the summer heat and the mosquitoes. Most of them have rocking chairs on them. Tucked back along the Sound, in the deepest patch of woods on the Outer Banks, Kitty Hawk Village is probably much like it was at the turn of the century.

The woman the Reverend told us about is waiting on one of those carefully scrubbed porches. Mrs. Beacham isn't tall, but she's erect and neat in a maroon pantsuit. Her hair is so naturally curly it looks permed, her glasses are thick, and her mouth looks like it's done a lot of smiling in eighty-seven years.

"I was born over in Colington. I don't really know where my family came from. They were from Colington, that's all I know about them. My mother's family, she was a Green before she married.

"Well, the first thing I remember – I was born in 1901. And I don't know how old I was, but I remember my daddy and the other men sittin' on the edge of the porch talkin'. Sit there and whittle, that's about all there was to do, just hit on a stick, they didn't carve. And they tellin' about this fella that was going to make a flying machine, they called it. They said, 'Does he think people's going to fly, up in the air?' And they were really laughing about that, how silly he was.

"My daddy didn't live to see a lot of it. But I must have been awful small, because he died and I left there when I was seven. I think pneumonia, was what it was.

"And there was seven of the children and no money – there was no insurance or nothing. So we had to put some of them around in the family and like that. Some stayed home; my oldest brother was thirteen, I think, and he'd been fishing some with Daddy, he kept right on working and helping what he could; and then my oldest sister she worked same as I did.

"All my brothers and sisters are dead now. I've got two half brothers; one lives in Kitty Hawk and one lives in Colington. There was seven of the first set, when Daddy died, and then my mother married again and had two. And those are the only ones I got living.

"My daddy was Decatur Gaimel. He fished, like most everybody down here. He did the freshwater fishing and hunting, and killed waterfowl to eat and things like that.

Raised gardens. Corn, beans, squash, salad green, tomatoes, cucumbers. Most everybody raised a garden. And most of the men fished. If they didn't fish for a living they fished some to get fish for the family . . . course there was a lot of them in the Coast Guard out here. This beach, when I was little, there was no cottages on the beach, no houses at all except three cottages to each Coast Guard station. Sometimes be a fish camp in between, but no cottages. I remember that very well.

"Let's see . . . I remember they raised their hogs. And they had cattle. The cattle and the hogs were out loose in the woods. Down on the Moore shore, on the sound side of the beach. And if anybody wanted beef or pork they went and killed a cow or a hog. They were all marked, everyone had a mark of their own, on the ears. They'd go and kill a beef, and take it in the cart and drive to the neighbors all around and sell them a piece. It was mighty cheap. And they killed hogs every winter.

"Colington was the same way. They had their cattle and hogs loose in the woods, and they killed them if they wanted. And they cooked on a wood stove. You had to wash a pretty day because you had to dry your clothes outside. There was no running water; you had to go outdoors, pump your water. And the little house over the swamp we called the johnny.

"And there were no cars here at all. Anyone went anywhere, we had to go in a cart. And if we left Kitty Hawk we had to go by boat, 'cause there was no bridges.

"I saw the first car come to Kitty Hawk. There used to be a house across the road over there, and I was standing on the porch, and it was summertime. And we heard a roaring, from out where the cattle and hogs was out loose. And Mr. Zekey Midgett, he lived over there, he says, 'What is that roaring?' And then he said, 'I bet I know what it is. I bet it's a autymobile!" He said he heard that Lem Beasley at Duck had got an automobile. And by that time we could see the hogs and the cattle going in the swamp on both sides of the road. It weren't paved then, just dirt road. And then come this Model T chuggin' along down the road. And that were in 1919.

"So I was put over here at my aunt's in Kitty Hawk. She lived in the little house next to this one. I was only seven, but I helped with all the work. I helped with the dishes, and fixing the beds, and helped with the housework, same as every girl that was there. I don't even know and remember when I started cooking. I always watched how they cooked and how they did it.

"I started school after I come over here. It was over on the other side of the church down here, on that road we call the Baum Ridge; it was a little school, one room.

"I stayed Kitty Hawk until I was twelve. And after I was twelve, I didn't get any more school. I went out to look out for m'self.

"Housework was the only kind of work there was here for a woman. And they had plenty of that to do. I lived round with people who needed somebody to help them. I scrubbed the clothes on the board, I've still got my glass washboard, and heated flatirons on the wood stove to do the ironing. The floors were bare, and you scrubbed them with soap and water. Strong soap, Octagon. Melt it in hot water and scrub with it. With a crowd of kids it'd get dirty a lot and you had to scrub it every week. And some of 'em had mighty white, pretty floors. That's the way you scrubbed clothes, too, with melted soap. I've scrubbed the skin off my fingers a good many times, and they're crooked, yes.

"Ironin' was my worst chore, the whole way growing up. I loved to wash, and I loved to do the housework; I like to cook, I like to do any of it but iron. I didn't like that, it made me tired standing in one place.

"One day out of every week you had to scrub clothes on the board, do a big wash and wash all day. And then the next day, it didn't make any difference how hot it was, you had to have that wood stove running heat them irons, and you did your ironing. All the pillow slips were starched, and all the children's clothes were starched. It was a small iron, with a handle on to it. You had two or three of them on the stove and you'd take one and iron till it got too cool and put that back and take a hot one. Always had something to wipe the iron off, then you'd put wax on to it and then wipe it and then you'd iron.

"And sometimes Aunt Lottie, my daddy's sister, she had what she called a steamboat iron. She put coal in to it. There was little hills all along here then. And they leveled the hills and filled in the swamp to make the yard bigger. The swamp did come to the back of this house.

"And there was coal in them hills. Yes sir, coal. I don't know how it got there. But I helped them fill in the swamp. They had little carts and wheelbarrows, all but me, and they'd put the sand in and put it in the swamp. I'd take a washpan and fill it up, and that was heavy for a seven-year-old; and carry it and pour it in the swamp. But I stayed at it till they seen I was a good worker, and then they made me a wheelbarrow too.

"And savin' out every piece of that coal; sometimes there'd be a piece big as your head. Aunt Lottie would put that in her iron, and start a fire, and it would puff smoke out and she would iron with that. Called it her steamboat iron. That's the only one I ever saw.

"I think about it sometimes. I don't see how we could stick up to the work we had to do.

"When I was twelve I went back over to Colington for a while. Then different ones, Manteo, Manns Harbor, would need someone to help them. Maybe a tiny baby comin' round or something. And I'd help look after the little children.

"I remember when I stayed in Manteo with the Etheridge Midgetts, his wife was sick in bed and they had six children. And I had to cook and clean and there was two or three of them in school. I was maybe fourteen or fifteen by then. I got eight dollars a month. I got a place to stay and something to eat, so all I had to do was buy my clothes. I didn't get a chance to go anywheres much, but the ladies was willing for me to use the sewing machine, and would show me how to buy material and cut out a dress and make it. And I made children's clothes. I never did know how to make clothes for the boys, but I sewed for the five girls, and I cut their hair.

"No, I wasn't treated like a servant. I was just like one of the family. When I was working there they called me 'Inez.' Inez I. Gaimel's the way it was before I was married. I know there's the I. but I don't know if there's anything else there or not. I've not spelled my name so long I don't know exactly how you spell it. Now in Kitty Hawk they called me Miss Inez. The children – they wanted the children to learn to work, too, so we'd work together; maybe one'd wash dishes and the other'n dry them. And the lady, if she wasn't sick, she went ahead about her work, and I went ahead doing whatever I had to do.

"Now they call them maids, I guess, but then it was just 'hired girl.' Everybody was trying to get hold of me and my sister. And any other of the girls around that needed to work, why there's somebody always after us. We'd hear of somebody from Manns Harbor come over looking for help, and we'd go.

"One place I went, Mashoes Creek, I didn't stay but a week there. They kept post office, and all the water we had was from tar barrels, to catch the rainwater off the roof, and it had to sit there in the hot sun all day. And we had fried salt herrings every morning for breakfast. I didn't like them so much, especially when I had to drink hot water from the tar barrels. You know how tar smells, that taste is just like it.

"No, my aunt never told me what to do if someone got fresh. People didn't talk about things like it at all. I lived one place in Manteo, and I'd heard that this lady had had girls to live there she was jealous of. And I was so scared she was going to be jealous of me I didn't know what to do. One day, it was in the spring, we took the stove down. Her husband and myself took it out in the barn. And her and the children stayed on the porch.

"Well, I made sure he went in first, with his side of the

stove, and when I got my side of it in I backed right out and ran for the house hard as I could. He liked to tease . . . he come back and said to his wife, 'I wouldn't have stayed so long, but I couldn't get her out of there; I thought she never would leave.'

"The most I made was at Poyner's Hill, that was twenty-five dollars a month. They wanted somebody to come up and cook for the men at the Coast Guard station. And I thought, I'll soon be rich at that. So I went up there. And Captain Yeoman lived next door to the kitchen, and his family had a girl about my age, and I stayed there nights with her; and mornings I'd get up before day and go over't the station, get to cooking. I was fifteen or sixteen, teen age girl.

"The first morning I cooked, they had hams hanging in the pantry, and I sliced ham and cooked it for breakfast. I did it the way we was always used to fixing it, we called it redeye gravy. We had to cook coffee in a big pot on the wood stove there. And I fried the ham, and put it in a bowl, and I poured coffee in that grease where I cooked the ham, and let it cook a little bit and poured it over the sliced ham. And I cooked biscuits. And at that time it was during the war, the first war, and they had dark flour and white flour. And I had to use half of the dark and half of the white because you couldn't get but so much of the white, and you had to make it go as far as you could.

"So I cooked breakfast, and I rang the bell, and they come in. And I was sittin' in there shaking, scared they were going to find fault and fire me.

"But when they finished eating they all went out but

Frank. He was what they called the Number One Man. My daughter, lives next door, married his son. He's been dead a long time. And he said, 'Steward, come here.' And I thought, boy, wonder what he's going to find fault with. He said, 'Would you tell me how you made that ham gravy?' I said, 'Made it with coffee. Isn't that what you're used to?' 'No,' he said, 'we had flour gravy.' And he said, 'Be sure and keep it up, everybody was crazy about it.' And he said, 'I never seen anybody make good biscuits with that dark flour before. But everybody said they were delicious.' So it made me feel better.

"But when I'd get a meal on the table I'd step out on the steps and ring the bell, and they'd come over from the station. And then I went in the pantry and closed the door. And I stayed in there until they left. And Frank would say, 'Steward, we're leaving.' And I'd come out when they all got out.

"Yes, they had a hot lunch; it was beans or peas, and some meats of some kind. But on Fridays we always had pumpkin pies. Up there, on the beach like that, I'd lose track of the days. But on Friday they put their pillows and their bedding out on the roof, out the window, and air them out over at the station. One time they decided to do that on Thursday, so when I saw that out on the roof I went to cooking. When they come over they had pumpkin pie. So when they all went out Frank said, 'Well, steward, course they's just as good on Thursdays as they are on Fridays, but how come you cooked pies on Thursdays?' I said, 'You put your linens to air out today, didn't you?' And he said, 'Yes, we changed.' I said, 'So did I.'

"Supper was about the same, we had fish and corn bread and things like that.

"No, they didn't flirt with me. They was just as nice. They didn't come over to the kitchen at all. Only to eat, when I rang the bell.

"Then I went to Norfolk. It was right after the First World War. I was about eighteen, I guess. My stepbrother was on a tugboat up there, and some friends of his, they needed a girl. And they asked him if he could get somebody to come help them out for a little while.

"So I went and I lived with this lady in Berkley till her baby was a month old. And she had three or four other children. And she said, 'Inez, I can't afford to hire you no longer, but I wish you'd get a job here. I'll give you a place to stay, and your board when you're off, just help me out anytime you can. Because I don't want you to leave.' I said, 'I don't know my way around here in Norfolk.' She said, 'I'll look in the paper, and I'll get you a job.' So she looked in the paper, and they'd just opened a cigarette factory. Well, with not much education, something like that's all I could handle. She took me over there and I got the job. And I worked the night shift; they had all they wanted in the daytime.

"They weren't sold here; one kind was Pinheads. I never heard tell of that before or since. They're real strong. These were sent off somewhere, they made them for some other country. It was over in Norfolk, way out Granby Street, like you were going to Ocean View. So I had to catch a streetcar home from the factory. Go to Monticello Avenue and transfer to the other streetcar to Berkley. Get off at Berkley Avenue then I had to walk about three blocks to get home.

"And I worked there till I got married, at nineteen. His name was Roy Beacham. He was from Kitty Hawk and his people had moved to Berkley. I knew of him, but I was so small when I lived here I don't know if I ever spoke to him. He quit his job to get married, they wouldn't let him off, so then I worked three weeks and by then he had a job and I quit.

"He worked to a machine shop, at Old Dominion Shipyard, on boats; then when he left there he went as an engineer on General Mitchell's yacht. Yes, General Billy Mitchell. We've got a letter from him. I ran across it the other day. He wrote to my husband to get sailor suits for wear on the boat.

"He went south in the winter, to Florida, and north in the summer. And they'd stop in Elizabeth City for two or three days, and he'd come home, and then he'd go on again. And then after he left there he went to another boat; Dr. Alexander, I believe his boss's name was. So I had to raise the children by myself.

"I lived in Norfolk till my oldest girl was twelve, in 1933. I liked it all right till they started breaking in places up there, and I got scared, alone with six little children; I couldn't sleep. So I moved back in down here, and I bought the little house I was raised in, and had one more child here. And then later on built the bigger one.

"Since I've been living here I've had six children in school at one time. And I had nineteen hogs in a pen. I'd take the kids, when they'd get out from school, when I needed straw for hogs' beds. You'd take tow bags, burlap bags, and a rake and go up this ridge back the house and bring back bags of straw. I had a big pound there, but I had a smaller pen and that's where I put the straw, you see, with a door they could go in, and a shelter over 'em. And they'd all go in there and sleep in straw beds, didn't have to lay on the cold ground. And I don't know how many chickens, I had a big chicken house out here and I sold some. Most of them were Plymouth Rock.

"And I'd have hog killings. I'd put out word to the neighbors to come help me. And they killed the hogs, and the womenfolks would come and help with the sausage and salting the hams and shoulders. The first thing I moved in this house was smoked hams and shoulders, hung 'em in my pantry, 'cause they smelled so good.

"My husband's boss, Dr. Alexander, he was a huge man. He come here once. And he said, 'Miz Beacham, what time you get up mornings?' And I said, 'Four o'clock.' And my husband told him about the nineteen hogs, and the chickens, and six children. He said, 'I don't know how you do it, Inez.' And he turned to my husband and he said, 'I didn't know you were buildin' a new house.' And my husband said, 'I know you didn't.' He said, 'I know why you didn't tell me. You were afraid I'd offer some help. And I would have. If you'd have told me you were building a house you'd have had the nicest house in Kitty Hawk.' And when he went back to the boat he sent me a check.

"My husband said many times he didn't know how I kept going.

"The children was in school then; and they was real smart. They'd come home evenings and help me cook supper. Do anything they could. I raised them to work, same as I was always used to doing. I was strict with them.

"My youngest daughter and her youngest girl was here not long ago and she said that her girl was doing that clog dancing, I don't know what you call it, anyway she looked real cute in her outfit, and she let her go with them, the school bunch, you know; but then she heard that sometimes they took them to bars and things, and she stopped it right then. Took her out of it. And my daughter said, 'I knew you wouldn't to let me do nothing like that.' And I said, 'No, I wouldn't.' But I don't know, she's sixteen, and she's never let her go out on a date yet. And I said, 'Well, she's a young girl, she's got to date some.' She said, 'She'll date right in the living room, that's where we courted.'

"No, I don't know much about the war. We read a paper once in a while, read about it. If I got time. Now I can't do much reading; my eyes is going bad fast.

"My husband always worked, right through the Depression. I don't remember when he stopped yachting, but I went and told him I was tired of raising the children by myself, and for him to come home. And he came home. The first job he got was cooking at the Kitty Hawk Coast Guard Station. Then he got a job on the pilot boat in Norfolk. He was out at sea two weeks, then he'd come home stay a week. He went on the pilot boat till his health went bad; then he retired.

"My daughter, the Shannons, we come in together. We had a little store down the road here. Grocery store, it used to be Mr. Jesse Baum's store, and we bought it from him. And she run the store, with her husband, and then there were some other women who worked there; and they all come up here and got their dinner at twelve o'clock every day. I kept their two boys, and I cooked for them all, and I did the washing for them all. So it was quite a crowd to eat.

"We saved what we could, and then we built a motel down at the beach. The Sea Cove. It's still there. We started it up with four apartments, and we had twelve when my husband died. My daughter and I did the washing, all the linens and that. We had a little washroom back of the place, and a washing machine, and I dried the clothes on the line. We stripped the beds, we fixed the beds, we washed the linens and ironed them, cleaned the bathrooms, cleaned all of it. Bill Foreman has it now.

"I'll be eighty-seven fourteenth of December. I don't get around good as I used to, but I'm getting round better'n most of them my age anyway. This knee joint is about wore out; I can't bend it up as far as the other one, and if I sit too long, I can't get around good for a few minutes. I had arthritis in it so bad I had acupuncture treatment. It sure helped me.

"I don't know why we're here. Anyway, long as I can help in some way I want to stay. When I can't help, then I'm ready to go. I keep house for my two sons. My oldest son's retired from the Coast Guard, he's up at his shop now, he loves to work on the boats and the engines and so on. He keeps all the cars up in the family. Well, I keep house. I won't say it's sparkling but . . . then if I don't have nothing else to do I do a little painting.

"Yes, these are all my paintings. When you drove up I was

looking at some pictures I was going to paint. I like to paint mostly geese, ducks. We're sitting a little too long, let's get up and look at them.

"Now this is when I lived with the Austins in Manteo, and sometimes we'd go down to Bodie Island and stay two or three days in this building next to the lighthouse. And that's gulls over there. That's March flowers there. It's oil, yes.

"I just paint whatever I'm thinking of. I never learned how but I was always drawin'. That's why they wanted me to go to the art class. When I was eighty my daughter signed me up at the school house and I took a course for a little while. I enjoyed being up there with the girls, I call them girls but they was all old women. I was the oldest there. They want me to go back but it's too much trouble . . . this is Saint Andrew Church, down the beach; and you've heard of Martin's Point. The art lady wanted us to paint that old house before they burned it down. That was about five years ago, I reckon.

"These are Canada geese. That's the kind I like to paint. I'll go, if I don't want to paint, then I'll make quilts or things like that. To pass away the time. Then I'll wake up some morning and I'll think of one them pictures I want to paint, and then as soon as I'm through with breakfast I'll start it.

"But I have to paint on a sunshiny day, when it's warm enough I can paint on the porch. I can't see good now. Have to have a lot of light. I had this eye operated on and it was damaged with age; and they said that this other one needs operated on too, but they didn't advise it, because I can see out of that better than the one I had operated on.

"That one's of Hatteras Light.

"The redbird, but I got to put some dark on his wings.

"More geese. I don't know why, I just love them, I think they're pretty.

"Lilac flowers. I wondered how you could paint lilac flowers, then I saw one day on television a girl was painting; and she put the purple on the brush and went this way, this way, this way.

"A beach scene. I got that from a calendar, I think.

"This is one of my quilts. It's a star quilt, I guess. Yes, I did this all by hand. I've made quilts for all my children, and a good many of my grandchildren. When I had the dining room in here I kept my quilting frame back of the sofa; and I'd sit there and watch television in the nights, and I'd be quilting; and in the daytime, when I wa'n't busy, when I sit down to rest I'd sit down to the quilting. No, didn't waste a minute. When you're my age you can't! I think it's best to stay busy. I just loved to work, and it seemed like that was all there was to do, was work. I never saw nothing else to do.

"I got seven children, I got twelve grandchildren, and I got nineteen great-grandchildren, and I got three great-great-grandchildren. One of them's running around pretty good, and the other two's too young to get around yet.

"I don't know when was happiest. Must have been after I was married and before my husband went off on the boats. When he worked at the shipyard, and he was home every evening. To a hot supper, and I'd cook hot biscuits for his breakfast; he'd go to work at seven-thirty; and he liked hot biscuits, so I'd cook them for him every morning. It wasn't very happy after he was gone, and it was just me and the children, but I never thought much about it.

"No, I think if I had it to do over again, I'd do it same as I been doing it. There might be some I'd do different. But I've got a nice large family, and I've enjoyed them. On Sunday evenings there's eight or ten or more here, and on Thanksgiving or Christmas I have all the way from twelve to fifteen. I usually do all the cooking, but last Christmas the girls didn't want me to; they did a lot of it and brought it in.

"I hate to leave, 'cause I think I'm needed here to keep house. I can find a lot to keep me occupied. I told my grandson, he's part owner at Owens, 'You know, I hope I live to be a hundred, if I'm still able to wait on myself. And if I do, I'm coming down here to Owens Restaurant, and I'll bring all my gang down here, we're going to have a ball, we're going to have a feast, all of us together.' Then I said, 'But I can't do that, 'cause you don't keep open till the fourteenth of December.' He says, 'Grandma, if you live to a hundred, we'll open it up, and you bring all your crowd down here.'

"Well, I don't know but one that's older than I am in Kitty Hawk, but I don't know if she's able. But I've told you how it was. I don't think there's much more to it. Weren't very good living around here, but we all got along. Better than it is in cities, where there's so much killing and such going on. We never heard of nothing like that down here.

"That's what's wrong with being this old. You know you can't live much longer. But I'll make good, I'll paint just as hard as I can as long as I'm here, anyway.

"Well, I've talked your ears off, and I know it's bad, the way I've been runnin' my mouth. But it's not half as bad as I'm going to tell my daughter for sending you over here. I told her I didn't remember anything. She said to go ahead, tell him what you know. I've already got my yarn ready, what I'm going to tell her I told you.

"Well, I've got to get going, get some supper for my boys, my little boys."

AFTERWORD

Now that you've shared eight lives with us, let's sit for a moment and reflect.

We have no intention of telling you what to think, or "interpreting" what you've just read. But we do ask you to ponder for just a moment. (And the younger you are, perhaps the more you might reflect.) What values have sustained these people through seventy or eighty years of life? How have they used them to meet the losses and sadnesses that confronted them?

And finally, what have they concluded about their lives? Did they find them worthwhile? What did they find most important – today's values of success and fame, or the quieter, more traditional values of family, friendship, work, and religion?

Obviously America has changed since 1900. For many readers, the circumstances and trials these people faced may seem dated and limited. But wait a moment. Do not the same evils afflict all lives, still; do not we too face illness, death, the thousand tribulations to which the flesh is heir? Perhaps today's mores have changed, as have the standards we set for ourselves. But these eight have endured through war and privation. They've survived, and, most of them, kept their independence and self-reliance. These are the survivors of generations past. In the final accounting, these are stories of success.

Working with them, listening to them, has led us to take a closer look at the priorities in our own lives. Their courage and nobility have inspired us and changed us. We hope they help you too.

More On Method

We gave in the Introduction a brief overview of how we located and interviewed our sources. For those who are interested in the processes of oral history, or who might like to do some of their own, here's a little more detail on the process.

Locating sources isn't an intrinsically difficult process, but it can be touchy. Immersed as we were in the life of the Banks through ten years of writing about it, we knew lots of people. But not all old folks like to talk. Most are modest, even reclusive. They have no especial ambition to see their names, and those of their relatives, in print. Others feel, for various reasons, that their reminiscences are private matters, best restricted to family gatherings.

Approaching them was thus a delicate matter, and we'd like to thank, again, those family members, friends, and clergymen who helped us gain their trust. For those interested in helping preserve our oral traditions, our advice is: do it, do it now, but do it gently and carefully. Respect your sources. They deserve it – and you'll get better material that way.

We met with each person we interviewed several times.

At the initial meeting we introduced ourselves and explained the project. If they agreed to continue, we'd then set up a cassette recorder. This tends to make some people nervous, but most of them get over it. Reassure them that they'll have a chance to correct your transcript personally, and that nothing they say will be printed without their agreement.

Following each interview came the most painstaking and time-consuming stage: transcription. We played tapes five times, eight times, to make sure what we typed was what was said, not what we thought was said, or "should" have been said. In questionable cases we placed brackets around transcripted material, to remind us to check this carefully with the source.

We then asked each man or woman to read the typed transcript. (Or, if this was difficult for them, we read it aloud, pausing after each sentence for concurrence or disagreement.) Together we corrected misstatements, mishearings, and spelling errors, usually of local names. Often this triggered new memories, which we then added or incorporated. This process was taped as well.

In the next stage we "boiled" the transcript down. This took a great deal of midnight oil. We took out the redundancies, the nonessentials, condensing it into a more readable form while at the same time retaining facts and opinions of even marginal interest.

Combined with this was a minimal amount of correcting grammar and syntax. Now, there's a tradition (The Marilyn Daniels Midgett interview refers to this) that the dialect spoken in the Outer Banks is Elizabethan English. This is a matter for linguists. Personally we'd believe that more readily of Tangier Island, in the Chesapeake. But you will hear a distinctive, older form of our language in these pages. It's not Standard American, but it's not *wrong*. The use of the double negative as an intensifier is an example; Shakespeare used it; the way some of our sources use it is no different.

The final transcript was checked again with the source. There was usually very little to change at this point.

There have been no changes in the years since. The interviews you have just read are presented exactly as they were approved by the sources.

The original tapes are now in the custody of the Outer Banks History Center in Manteo, North Carolina, where they may be accessed by researchers.

On the Old, Everywhere

Most American families today are "nuclear" families: mother, father, children; and a growing number are even less "traditional." But we're not sure you can call them "families" if there isn't an older person around. Certainly in most human societies, and for most of American history too, you couldn't.

The Outer Banks still lags in the modern atomization of the family. Oddly, though their people appear strong and self-reliant as individuals, the extended family lingers. On these islands people still live in houses with white picket fences; they still go to church; and they still take care of their old people. It's worth remarking that most of our sources – those who aren't still fending for themselves, like Inez Beacham and

Ernal Foster – were being cared for in their own homes, by their own people. The traditions you'll find described in this book are not gone. They are still carried on. And we think they'll still be there fifty years from now.

We love these men and women. We've been enriched by their stories in a way that is deeply felt but hard to define. It's the culmination of a long ambition to share them with you.

If you have old folks, don't neglect them. Honor them. We each must make our own choices. But they've travelled the hard roads before us; they know them better than we. They will help us, if we will only listen. They're resources. They're treasures. We owe them everything.

And at the end, this book is a tribute to them – those who made our world for us, and who made us what we are.

THE END

About the Author

David Poyer is a nationally known novelist with close ties to the Outer Banks of North Carolina. Millions of copies of his thirty-plus books are in print, including national bestsellers and such favorites as *The Return of Philo T. McGiffin, The Threat, The Command, The Crisis, The Towers,* (St. Martin's Press) and a Civil War at Sea Trilogy that begins with *Fire on the Waters* (Simon & Schuster). Along with this book, Northampton House has republished his four Hemlock County novels, *The Dead of Winter, Winter in the Heart, As the Wolf Loves Winter,* and *Thunder on the Mountain,* and also his sea adventures starring Hatterasman Tiller Galloway: *Hatteras Blue, Bahamas Blue, Louisiana Blue,* and *Down to a Sunless Sea.* His latest book is *The Whiteness of the Whale.* Poyer lives on Virginia's Eastern Shore with his wife and daughter, and teaches in the Creative Writing Program at Wilkes University, Wilkes-Barre, Pennsylvania.

Northampton House Press

 Northampton House Press specializes in carefully selected creative nonfiction, memoir, poetry, and fiction. Our mission is to discover great new writers and give them a chance to springboard into fame. See our list at www.northampton-house.com, or Like us on Facebook–"Northampton House Press"–to discover more innovative works of high quality from brilliant new writers.

Made in the USA
Charleston, SC
06 July 2014